HOW TO WIN

at

STUD POKER

By James M. Wickstead.

The Author wishes to acknowledge, with grateful appreciation, the help along historical lines received from the following sources—

The British Museum.

Facts and Speculations on the Origin and History of Playing Cards, by William Andrew Chatto.

United States Playing Card Company.

Brown & Bigelow.

Association of American Playing Card Manufacturers.

Other sources are credited where used.

⚬↯⚬

Gambler's Book Club

Las Vegas, Nevada 89106

⚬↯⚬

*"Happy the man who, studying
nature's laws
Through known effects can trace
the secret cause."*

Virgil.

INTRODUCTION TO G.B.C. EDITION

This G.B.C. Gambling Classic Reprint is one of the more scholarly works on the Great American Game—Poker. J. M. Wickstead observes the game in three ways: as an astute mathematician, as a psychologist and as a player. A book that has long been out of print, but continuously requested by our customers, it will give an insight into the game of Stud that will aid any devoted player, regardless of the brand of Poker played. In fact, Wickstead's analysis of Poker can be applied to all card games. With little adjustments, his theory of "Net-Odds" will gain points for all players of Gin, Pinochle, Bridge, Cribbage—you name it.

Ponder the paragraph on Page 49 starting, "The gambler bets—the sucker calls," and believe the author. The player who gets the money has learned this axiom very well.

Even though it has nothing to do with the play of good Poker—Good Luck, anyway"

G.B.C.

CONTENTS

THE BRIDGE WORLD
INCORPORATED
570 Lexington Avenue
New York, N. Y.

Cable Address "BRIDGEWORLD"

January 31, 1933

Mr. James Wickstead
1823 Alfresco Place
Louisville
Kentucky

Dear Mr. Wickstead:

Thank you for your very scholarly
and complete analysis of the game of poker.

It is indeed unfortunate that this
kind of psychological game has, as you say,
"no court of last resort."   And thus, to
quote the ancient Hebraic judges, "each man
does that which is right in his own eyes."

Sincerely yours,

Ely Culbertson
Editor-in-chief
The Bridge World.

[Mr. Culbertson's valued answer
to a letter from the author.]

FOREWORD.

It has been said that, in the natural order, there are only two true sciences, mathematics and music. You will find no music in this book but you will find plenty of math. If you think, for one moment, that poker is not subject to the laws of chance and probability then this book is not for the likes of you.

On the other hand if you can see, in the fall of the cards, an observance of well defined principles and desire to learn more about this interesting phenomena this book should prove helpful. If you can take your arithmetic or leave it, and elect to leave it, you should find lots of information in the chapters on the history and philosophy of cards well worth your while.

"How to Win At Stud Poker" was first published in 1938 and much of its material will be found in this new issue. After this new volume was written the subject of the title of the new book presented itself. The decision to continue the same designation was based on two reasons, the words "How to Win" are not misleading and, in addition, they are founded on a fundamental desire of human nature.

In presenting it to the public, while I invite criticism, I offer no apology because I believe that it contains a message to stud players and ask for the book continued good will. I feel that it deserves a place in the library of anyone interested in a game so universal in scope in its social and scientific features as to be equally appealing to both the emotions and intellects of men. Stud poker can justly be called the leaven of the masses and the joy of scholars.

In my opinion there is nothing like the game of poker for speeding up the "revolutions of the psyche."

May I suggest that the eager mind will find in this book, as also in its predecessor, the first original thoughts on poker since the introduction of jack pots and the draw?   WICK.

A Short History of Cards In General and Stud Poker In Particular

"Came you from the King, my lord?
I did, Sir Thomas; and left him at
primero
With the Duke of Suffolk."

> Act V, Scene 1.
> King Henry VIII.

It has always been my thought that poker is a Royal game, really, the sport of or at least one of the sports of Kings.

The above quotation from Shakespeare would seem to bear out the idea as primero is one of a long list of similar diversions from which the modern game of poker is derived.

I have no thought of placing poker's ancestors in any particular sequence, nor of going into detail regarding their peculiarities but am merely trying to place before the reader a few facts concerning a game which is deserving of at least a little critical investigation.

However, before studying the history of stud poker let's examine the broader aspect of playing cards and endeavor to trace, in a general manner, their progress through the centuries in which they have had an existence as the subject is very interesting.

Even though there is much conjecture in the story of cards, and I have done my share of conjecturing in regard to their philosophy, I am not conscious of having garbled accepted data. My conclusions are based on evidence, which, if not indisputable, is, in my opinion, certainly at least admissible. In this connection it may be said that the reader of a book has a certain advantage over the writer, he reads and believes only those things that he finds interesting or that are to his liking.

Despite the fact that the assignment has its rewards, the role of the conscientious historian is not always a happy or an easy one. By the nature of the task, his lot in life is to record, with reportorial accuracy, all those things that come within the scope of his agency or research. When he essays the duty of reasoning why such things have come to pass, he steps out of character, as it were, and enters the realm of philosophy.

For example, when the writer on the subject of cards tells you that the king of diamonds and the jacks of hearts and spades are shown in profile, only; and have been, for years; he has done his duty as the historian. When he attempts to tell you why these court cards are so shown, he plays the role of the philosopher.

Long ago, historians learned that the best way to recall the piquancy of an age, the tang of a people, is by reading the newspapers, books and private letters of the time. To these sources of information might also be added playing cards.

The playing card is the product of the middle ages, a period of history profoundly meditative, the works of the artisans of the time showing a decided leaning toward those spiritual and mystical values of life so often overlooked by civilizations more materialistically inclined. The playing card, a subject of enchanting interest, should be interpreted in the light of the spirit of the age in which it was born, a feudalistic, medieval age founded on a handicraft commerce, rather than one founded on machinery, it is the product of an age when man was happier, psychically.

It is easy to understand the lasting impression created by playing cards, these fascinating mementoes of a time in history now little known or understood, when we realize that the age that gave them to us, was the one that also gave to the world such original thinkers as Stephen Langton, Edward the First, "the English Justinian;" Roger Bacon, Giotto, Dante and that gigantic intellect, the "Angel of the Schools," St. Thomas Aquinas.

Despite these obvious facts, I have no desire, nor do I think it germane, to try to trace the growth of the playing card from its inception as its birth is too obscure. Its almost legendary introduction into Europe, possibly by returning Crusaders during the 11th, 12th or 13th Centuries, or maybe by the Moors through Spain at an earlier date, opens a field of dissertation much too broad to be confined within the covers of a book bearing the title "How to Win At Stud Poker."

However, I am sure that a few comments on the history of the modern card will not be doing the reader an injustice, so I make them in order that poker players may become better acquainted with a most interesting phase of Americana, which, if not recorded here might escape them altogether. I also have a desire to be precise in my treatment of the subject.

During the middle ages, the four suits represented the four main classes of people—the nobility, the clergy, the merchant and the peasant, represented, respectively, by the symbols of swords, cups, coins and staves. These symbols gave way to spades, hearts, diamonds and clubs about the middle of the 15th Century, and even though at different times the four suits have been pictured in other designs, the present ones seem to have been the most popular and lasting.

It may be said that cards of freakish design, educational in character, or those depicting remarkable events have never been popular with regular card players. They seem to have the tendency to divert the attention of the player from the game.

Prior to the adoption of its present dress, that is, about the beginning of the 16th Century, the playing card experienced many vicissitudes, each age having the desire to leave its mark on the cards printed at that time. The dress of the court cards was also changed from time to time, consistent with the whims of reigning monarchs as card manufacturers always thought it wise to reflect the tastes of the ruling King and Queen. This is particularly true of cards of a Continental European origin. In later years, those of English make maintained their designs far more consistently.

Not only did each epoch endeavor to leave its mark on the cards manufactured at the time, but every country in which they made their appearance also stamped its cards with ideas and dress peculiar to itself.

Unquestionably, however, the stability of the design of the modern playing card leads one to believe that of all the inheritances from the age of chivalry, it is probably the most truly representative in that it has been the least affected by the ravages of time. Mute though its testimony be, it remains an indissoluble link between our modern, mechanical age and the time "when knighthood was in flower."

It is interesting to note that although practically all nations possessing cards personified them to a certain extent, France, where their actual history begins, seems to have been most successful in giving to cards names which have been preserved more consistently and which are familiar to more people than those bestowed by other nations.

For example, the kings in the pack were named in honor of Charlemagne, Alexander, David and Caesar, for hearts, clubs, spades and diamonds, respectively. The queen of hearts was Isabel, wife of Charles VI of France. Mary of Anjou, wife of Charles VII was queen of clubs. Joan of Arc was queen of spades and the fair Agnes Sorel, a favorite of Charles VII, was queen of diamonds.

The celebrated Etienne de Vignoles, surnamed La Hire, said to have been the inventor of the game of piquet was the jack of hearts and the jack of clubs was Lancelot, a paladin of the court of Charlemagne. Ogier the Dane, a medieval character of great renown was jack of spades and Hector de Garlard, captain of the Guard to Louis XI of France was jack of diamonds.

France endowed its cards with these names, prominent in history, which seemed to illustrate best the various qualities for which the people wanted the court cards to stand. Giving the court cards names also helped preserve the memory of these historical personages and at the same time had a tendency to inspire a national solidarity and mutual understanding which otherwise, might have been sadly lacking.

Even though the playing card is not an original product of England; it probably having been taken there, through French influence, by soldiers returning from the Hundred Years War which began in 1338; and the four suits used, likewise being of foreign importation into Britain, we in the United States use cards that have been thoroughly Anglicized in appearance. England started making her own cards sometime during the 15th Century but even prior to this time the cards manufactured for the English trade bore characteristics near and dear to the heart of the Briton.

It may be said that the kings in the English pack were not like their less fortunate brothers in France, in that they never lost their heads. When Benjamin Franklin suggested the phrase "Liberty, equality, fraternity" as the watch word of the French revolution, little did he think that the purge would extend to playing cards, also. But it did, and the sovereigns in the pack were soon replaced by popular figures of the time. Although cardboard Royalty was eventually restored, for quite a number of years French cards showed unmistakable evidence of the volatile capriciousness of the Gaul.

The study of cards discloses the interesting fact that from the time of Henry VIII of England, who ascended the throne in 1509, the kings in the English pack have been garbed like "bluff King Hal." Possibly reminiscent of his attire when meeting Francis 1 of France on "The Field of the Cloth of Gold." The queens represent his mother, Elizabeth, of York.

The sanguinary Wars of the Roses ended in 1485 when Henry, Earl of Richmond, a Lancastrian, ascended the English throne as Henry VII, the first of the Tudor kings. He married Elizabeth of York, uniting the Houses of York and Lancaster and brought peace to a country that had been torn asunder by fratricidal strife for more than thirty years. Much in the same manner that we in America issue stamps (and playing cards) to commemorate historical events, the thoroughgoing English saw fit to have the kings and queens in their packs garbed in regalia that would have a tendency to keep the people ever mindful of the union that had finally been achieved.

Henry VIII, son of Henry VII and Elizabeth, extremely popular with his people, was chosen as the model for the king and his mother for the queen. The rose in the queen's hand is the pale rose of York.

Both English and American cards attest to this historical event and from that time have been daily reminders, in the lives of countless thousands, of the wars of almost five centuries ago.

Four nations played a most important part in the settlement of early America, Spain, England, France and Holland. All four countries had playing cards of their own, and, although undoubtedly the playing card was introduced into America by the Spaniard, by far, the ones most popular in the United States are those of distinctly English origin. This fact is no doubt due to the thoroughness with which the English made their presence felt in early American history, and the influence exerted by the Anglo-Saxon on American Colonial life.

Theodore Roosevelt, in his remarkable history, "The Winning of the West," goes into detail regarding the different methods of colonizing used by those European nations that battled for supremacy in the New World. He states that when countries, other than England, moved into a new land, there was no great displacement of native populations. These nations simply sat down where they found themselves and were practically absorbed by their surroundings.

This was not so when England took a hand in the proceedings.

In early American history, the story of the growth of our country is bound up more in the story of the wars of the invaders among themselves, rather than in the story of the wars of the invaders with the aboriginal inhabitants. The Englishman finally prevailed and it is from England that most of the ideas along cultural and social lines now prevalent in the United States have come. Therefore, it is most natural that our playing cards, too, should bear unquestionable evidence of English derivation and there is no reason to believe that they will not continue to preserve their present form, possibly, until that time in the dim, distant future when Macaulay's traveler "from New Zealand shall, in the midst of a vast solitude, take his stand on a broken arch of London Bridge, to sketch the ruins of St. Paul's."

Catherine Perry Hargrave, in her book, "A History of Playing Cards and a Bibliography of Cards and Gaming" quotes Shakespeare as referring to a "deck" of cards but that nowadays to call a "pack" a "deck" is a provincialism of the States in the Mississippi and Ohio River Valleys, according to the British Museum in a catalogue published in the eighteen-seventies.

Whether you call it "pack" or "deck," to me, seems to be of no special moment. What is important is the fact that playing cards have been, and are, sources of entertainment with hardly an equal in the ability to stimulate the mind.

With the hope that I have qualified the playing card

as a subject worthy of your attention; and that the evidence concerning it has been presented in a manner convincing enough to prove that it occupies no trivial place in history; we will now consider the definite spot that stud poker holds in the lives of millions of people.

The game of stud poker, with its advent about the year 1870 although its genesis is clouded in obscurity, comes down to our time through a list of progenitors containing the names Brag, Primero, Post and Pair, As Nas and Poque, the last named probably being the one from which "Poker" is taken.

Not in any "apostolic succession," however, as the line of cleavage is too loosely drawn to permit anyone to say just when one game was succeded by the other.

According to the best information that we have, modern or straight poker dates from about the year 1830. A popular magazine of that time contains a description of a game of poker played on a river steamer and from that time on, the game took such a hold on both the hearts and minds of men that its praises have been sounded "from border to border and coast to coast." Knowing no frontier, it has been internationally accepted and wherever men are gathered together, or women, either, the game of poker finds a ready welcome.

Edmond Hoyle was born in 1672 and died in 1769, spending a long and fruitful life in the world of cards. His name is one to conjure with, a hallmark as it were. It is indelibly printed in the minds of men and whenever the urge to impress with more than usual emphasis presents itself, we use the expression, "According to Hoyle."

The ejaculation has been inducted into the vernacular and now even railroads are run "according to Hoyle"; banks, that is, some banks, are operated "according to Hoyle"; police beats are patrolled "according to Hoyle" and, "believe it or not," even newspapers (at least the one I work for) are run "according to Hoyle."

It is a pity that the game of stud poker was not known in Hoyle's lifetime, as, no doubt, his comments thereon would have made interesting reading.

In this treatise on stud I will try to avoid that verbosity which seems to be so characteristic of nearly all instructions on card playing and even though it has been said that comparisons are both odious and "odorous," also undesirable, it is my contention that stud poker is a game, both scientifically and mathematically, the equal of any card game and in the following pages I hope to prove it, "come rack, come rope."

"To all those to whom these presents come," if they instruct an idle hour, I am content.

Luck, Chance and Probability In Their Relation to Cards and Gambling

The fundamental error in connection with luck is the belief that certain persons are lucky, antecedently, just because they have been the beneficiaries of several instances of good fortune. The fact that they have succeeded so far is certainly no evidence that they will continue to succeed indefinitely in matters of pure chance or of mingled chance and skill.

Therefore, it would be absolutely impossible for anyone to determine by trial and error, just what is and is not correct card playing. The amount of time that the individual can find to devote to the playing of stud poker is far too short to be able to establish any sound rules through inductive methods, alone. By far, the greater amount of our knowledge of how to play winning stud must be based on a proper mathematical understanding of the science of this fascinating game, secured deductively.

Chance and probability, in the world of cards, are indeed complex. In bridge, for example, there is a total of 635,013,559,600 hands in the 52-card and 648,045,936,942,300 hands in the 65-card packs, truly astronomical figures. How long would it take a player to examine a number of hands large enough to enable him to establish rules for expert play, based on experimentation? Likewise, one can see the futility of a mode of conduct in a stud game which demands that a player should play practically every hand! Don't pattern after the fellow who wanted "to go to all the weddings." See if you cannot find in this book the "peg" on which to hang calculations that will prove to be as sound in practice as they are in theory.

It has been said that "luck attaches to persons and not to things." If this statement be true, then our original thought on the subject, namely, that it is a fundamental error to think that persons are lucky, antecedently, is wrong. To say that "luck attaches to persons" (could it be because persons are articulate and "things" are not?) is practically tantamount to saying that one can be "sitting in the middle of a run of luck," which is absurd.

There is not a scintilla of scientific evidence to support the idea for instance, that just because a poker player filled or did not fill a flush at 9 P.M. the same thing will also happen at 9:10. Nothing that has previously happened in a game of chance can have any conceivable bearing on subsequent events. Every hand must be played as carefully as though it were the only hand to be played at that session. This carefulness can, of course, be carried to an extreme, but then, don't parade your thoughts on the subject before the crowd and none will be the wiser. Results will speak for themselves.

Generally speaking, in games of chance, a smart player need ask himself but one question, "Would I play it this way 100; 1,000; or 10,000 times?" The answer applies equally as well to the one time, they differ merely in degree, but not in kind. Learn to play the game correctly and then play it consistently, as without consistency, there can be no such thing as equalization of chances.

The writer was once sitting in a game of draw poker, in which, by actual count, he had the opportunity and desire to draw to fourteen flushes in the course of the evening's play. He filled twelve of them, pretty fair "hitting" in any man's league. Surely, no one would be childish enough to say that the "low man on a totem pole" would not have done the same thing. The inex-

16

orable hand of fate would certainly have dealt the same cards to anyone who happened to be in the same seat that this player was occupying. To think otherwise is equivalent to injecting the occult into the realm of cards and this is nonsensical, as cards are certainly impersonal in their likes and dislikes.

The only part the writer played in the making of the twelve out of fourteen possible flushes was to try to figure the odds in the pot in each case before the draw. The pot should always bet you an amount at least equal to the chance you are taking in the making of a hand. Granted that you never know in advance what it will cost to get "out," you should at least try to ascertain what it costs to get "in." Try to give yourself an "even break."

In stud poker you are hardly ever justified in backing a low hole card, for reasons explained in later pages. Likewise, the odds that the pot bets you are more likely to decrease than increase in your favor, as the play proceeds.

While there is no actual decrease in the odds that the pot bets you, the increase is not in direct proportion to the number of betting rounds. This "sluffing off" or downward gradation is due to players continually dropping out as play proceeds.

The rule is to figure the amount bet at any particular moment against the total amount in the pot at that time. The money that you have bet previously does not affect these odds as it belongs to the pot and is just as far removed as though it were in some other player's pile. Nor can you count on greater odds as there is no certainty that subsequent bets will be made. As far as that individual deal is concerned, it's "play or pay."

The very thing that would tend to increase the monetary odds in your favor, namely, the presence of additional players against you, would also probably serve to insure your defeat, this idea likewise being fully explained ·in subsequent pages. So, look the situation over carefully and check your hole card's value! If the odds against making a certain hand are, for instance, 4 to 1 and you get only 2 for 1 when you make this hand, it is easy to figure your losses in say, 100 or 1,000 such plays.

I have never heard of any "seventh son of a seventh son," who, for this reason alone, was particularly good at games of chance. To believe in "luck" is the sign of an ignorant man, enlightened men consider cause and effect. A player who must depend on "luck" or bluff in stud poker will make money much faster and easier by manufacturing stagecoaches or some other commodity equally obsolete. Changing the pack, the use of a talisman of some kind and other pet superstitions are just about as effective as "body english" on a bowling ball.

Changing your seat or care in choosing one's place at the table can very often be of practical value to a player, however. Try to sit as near to the left of a plunging type of player as you can, thus you are "behind" him in the betting and have a better chance to escape being caught by raises that may prove disastrous to you. When this plunging type bets heavily, drop out, unless your hand's value justifies your continuing.

The writer also was once sitting in a game of draw poker in which on one hand, he filled four kings. One of his opponents played his hand so skillfully and bet so strongly on it that all the author did, finally, was call, winning the pot, however. Needless to say, he will never be able to "live this down." But, then again, "good poker players are frequently bluffed."

Some of the biggest losses in poker are on hands that ordinarily would be considered almost invincible. Down South where the writer learned the rudiments of the game they always tell the old story about the lad who "lost a sawmill" drawing to a certain hand, finally made it and then "lost two sawmills" betting on it. So you never can tell.

Do not get the idea, however, that I think that stud poker can be successfully played only by mathematicians. I do not subscribe to this principle at all, but assuming that luck, over a period of time, is going to be more or less equally distributed and this is a reasonable assumption, there surely can be no harm in studying the fundamentals of cards and observing the rules by which they are governed.

I have never known a successful stud player who did not play his cards along sound mathematical lines, even though he may have been unaware of it. Unwittingly, perhaps, he observed those basic fundamentals so necessary even in a game of chance.

Chance is defined as—1, "The absence of any defined or recognized cause." 2, "An event which happens without any assigned cause," and is either for or against the event. Without delving too deeply in any vague form of transcendentalism but to give strength to arguments in favor of having and using certain knowledge pertaining to the mathematics of stud poker, it might be observed that, "It is strictly and philosophically true in nature and reason, that there is no such thing as chance or accident, it being evident that these words do not signify anything really existing, anything that is truly an agent or the cause of any event, but they signify merely men's ignorance of the real and immediate cause."

Probability is defined as—"Likelihood of the occurrence of any event in the doctrine of chances, or the ratio of the whole number of chances, favorable and unfavorable, to the number of favorable chances," and is always for the event. The chances are expressed by the fraction of this probability, the denominator being the total number of events possible and the numerator the number of events favorable.

The odds are found by deducting the favorable events from the total or the numerator from the denominator. For example, what is the probability of the number six coming up in a single throw of a die? There are six possible results, only one of which is favorable, therefore, the fraction 1/6 represents the probability of six being thrown on any particular occasion, or odds of five to one against it happening.

What is the probability that a seven will be thrown on any single roll of the dice? Seven can be made six ways: 6 + 1; 1 + 6; 5 + 2; 2 + 5; 4 + 3; 3 + 4; but the total number of events or numbers possible on a pair of dice is thirty-six, therefore thirty-six is your denominator and six is your numerator, hence the fraction 6/36 represents its probability. Odds against, 30 to 6 or 5 to 1.

What is the probability that the number four will be thrown on any particular throw of the dice? Four can be made in three ways, namely: 3 + 1; 1 + 3; 2 + 2; hence, three is the numerator and thirty-six, the same as before, is the denominator, the fraction 3/36 represents the probability of making a four on any single roll, odds against, thirty-three to three or eleven to one.

What is the probability that the number twelve will be thrown on any particular roll of the dice? Here we have only one chance out of thirty-six, as twelve can be made only one way; namely, 6 + 6; 1/36 is the fraction that expresses its probability, or odds of thirty-five to one against the number twelve showing.

You can see from the foregoing that while the denominator remains constant, the numerator fluctuates: it increases as the number of chances, favorable, increases and it decreases accordingly. As the number of favorable chances increases, the more closely the fraction of probability approaches unity or certainty.

We must remember, however, that there is a fundamental difference between dice and poker in the methods of figuring the chances of throwing certain numbers with dice and of being dealt certain hands from a pack of cards.

With dice there is no "diminution of substance" so the total number of possibilities or the denominator of the fraction of probability remains the same, the numerator increasing or decreasing consistently as the number of chances, favorable, increases or decreases.

In casting a die the fraction of probability illustrative of the chance of face ace showing is 1/6 and granted a perfect die, even in a successful run of nineteen consecutive aces the fraction 1/6, no more, no less, still represents the chance of the ace coming up on the twentieth roll, as the fraction of probability is a constant.

Not so in cards; in the following paragraph I have made a fair and accurate comparison between the chances of throwing five aces with five dice and of being dealt a pat spade flush from a deck of cards.

When you throw five dice the chance of rolling five aces is 1/6x6x6x6x6, 1/7776 or odds of 7,775 to 1 against all the aces showing but when you draw five cards from a pack there is an essential difference because each time you draw an additional card you draw from a depleted pack. The chance of drawing a spade from a full pack is 13/52; if that card is a spade the chance that the next card drawn will be a spade, there being but 12 spades left in the depleted pack of 51, is 12/51; if this also is a spade the chance of drawing a third spade is 11/50; for the fourth spade 10/49 and for the fifth spade 9/48.

Multipy these five fractions together and you have the chance of being dealt a pat spade flush; here is the arithmetic, 13/52x12/51x11/50x10/49x9/48 equals 154440/311875200; 311,720,760 to 154,440 or 2,018 to 1 against the hand. The chance is the same for each of the other three suits so the combined chances of being dealt any pat flush (including straight flushes) are four times that of any individual suit or about 504 to 1 against a hand of this denomination.

In experiments in the realms of chance and probability it is a fact that the deeper we explore these subjects, the more convinced we become that the laws on which they are based are sound, as both theory and practice are practically parallel in the long run. For example—of all the different possibilities in tossing a coin 10 consecutive times, that of 5 heads and 5 tails is the most probable, assuming of course that the coin is unweighted, the trial is fairly made and the dynamics of the test has not been outraged. It is entirely possible, however, that we might find heads turning up only one time and tails, nine, a most unusual division, but this unequal division will correct itself as the number of trails increases and you will find after repeated attempts that the fraction of deviation gradually approaches zero.

Again I say that in both the theory and practice of combinations and also in the realms of chance and probability, it is true that the deeper we explore these subjects the more convinced we become that the laws governing them are immutable.

In connection with both mathematics and card playing are two words which are of common usage but need strict defining if they are to be understood and properly applied. The words are "probability" and "frequency." When we say that the a priori probability, say, of six appearing when a die is cast is 1/6, we mean that the appearance of face six is one of six equally likely possibilities. If we use the same fraction to express the frequency of the appearance of face six, we should qualify the assertion by adding, "over a period of time," as although theoretically, the two words are synonymous, as a matter of practicality we often find them varying to a marked degree, as witness the series of long runs of some one number. Do not confuse the two words, merely mark their difference.

In playing stud poker, we are dealing with large numbers of facts of the same kind, therefore, frequencies, when subjected to the necessary precaution may be of great practical value. The certainty of great numbers must be of real worth as all large insurance underwritings are based on their correctness; however, we must realize that individual occurrences should be handled in a manner befitting the exigency and in the game of stud, regulate the play to suit the particular occasion. Uncertainty in the lot of the individual may be overcome to a great extent by proper knowledge of the frequency with which certain hands may be expected to appear in the course of play.

When an individual has a successful run in roulette the bank is enabled to stand the loss because of the soundness of the doctrine of frequencies. The bank deals in large numbers whereas the individual must content himself with certain probabilities which may or may not materialize at that particular time. In the case of the great majority of punters the capital of each is nearly always exhausted before the good results of frequencies begin to make themselves apparent.

This is the prime reason why, in stud poker, or in any game of chance, the limit should always be one that will not give certain players an advantage because of their better financial condition. Assuming that the technical knowledge of the game involved is equal, the player who can best afford to lose is most likely, eventually, to emerge winner. He is not playing "distressed money" and, as a result, can concentrate more closely on the game.

When Culbertson and Sims held their memorable joust at cards, some time ago, the total number of aces, kings and queens dealt during the tournament was 10,440. They were divided as follows:

	Sims	Culbertson
Aces	1751	1729
Kings	1765	1715
Queens	1784	1696
Totals	5300	5140

If 80 cards had been shifted from the Sims to the Culbertsons the distribution of the aces, kings and queens would have been absolutely even—a deviation of approximately 4/5 of 1% from equality, a most accurate and beautiful application of how the laws of probability work out over a period of time and we must remember that this period of time was relatively short, the two teams playing only 150 rubbers.

If the laws of average hold so accurately in a game where there are synthetic obstacles, where the nature of the play is so conducive to the overthrowing of these immutable "laws of nature," as it were, isn't it logical to conclude that in a game such as stud poker where there are no such artificial obstructions that the laws of chance and probability need but to be known and observed to be brought to a successful ending?

In stud poker in a 7 or 8 hand game the number of cards dealt out at any given time might vary from as low as 14 to as high as 40. The constant ebb and flow of the play would tend to shuffle the cards all the more and would practically guarantee that any resulting combinations would be due to chance and probability rather than to the innocent stacking of the deck by the players themselves.

Frequency distribution in cards varies greatly, but the basic ideas contained herein are sound. The distribution may at times seem distorted but you will be surprised to observe the extent to which probabilities hold good in stud. The flow of the cards is widely diffused, there is no "bottle neck" feature in the manner of playing, like that prevailing in bridge, for instance. The number of cards dealt in the course of play varies so much in successive deals that you can rest assured that stud is almost wholly mathematical and psychological.

In so far as ultimate realities are concerned, it

is most doubtful if there is any exact probability of anything. At the same time it is most important that we be able to distinguish between the events that are probable and the things that are most unlikely to occur. For example, the odds against making a flush in draw poker, on the draw, by drawing one card are 4 and 2/9 to 1, yet you may draw to 20 flushes and never fill one of them. There can be no such thing as certitude about future events when so-called "chance" is involved; there is merely a "reasonable probability."

It is the writer's opinion that a poker player should have a numerical measure to the probability of making the hand which he considers possible; otherwise, intelligent betting cannot be done. To illustrate the point let us consider the odds against making a flush in draw poker, as mentioned before, if on the deal you receive four hearts and a spade. In the unknown cards in the game, numbering forty-seven, are nine hearts; the fraction expressing the probability of your receiving a heart in the draw is 9/47; the fraction which expresses the probability of your not receiving a heart is 38/47. Therefore the odds against making the hand are 38 to 9 or 4 and 2/9 to 1 and you should get odds in the betting of at least this amount before the bet is a good one from a mathematical viewpoint.

It is also true that while the great difference between draw and stud poker is in the fact that in stud the known cards destroy the symmetry of the pack, yet the fractions of probability encountered in one are just as sound as those found in the other.

In order that we may find out more definitely what is meant when we say that the known cards destroy the pack's symmetry, consider a game of stud being played by 8 players. After the necessary shuffling and cutting, the deal starts. You are the player on the dealer's immediate left, the first one to receive a card. The card which is first dealt you, "in the hole," is an ace. Your first thought is, "Will I get them backed?"

Stop this theoretical deal after all players, including dealer, have been served and figure out your chance of being given another ace, as your first faced card.

There are 51 unknown cards among which are three aces. The fraction which expresses the probability that you will receive aces "back to back" is 3/51. The fraction which expresses the probability that you will not make the pair is 48/51. Odds against your making the pair are 48 to 3 or 16 to 1.

Supposing that you are the dealer, the last one to receive cards in this "laboratory test," how do the odds change? Continuing the deal around with each player being given a hole card and one up card, you find an ace in the hole—what is the chance that you will get them "back to back"? The fraction of probability has changed, it has been modified by the cards in sight. Assuming that no ace has been given to any player, showing, figure your chance of receiving an ace as your first up card.

You know the face value of each card showing in an opponent's hand plus your own hole card, a total of 8. There are 44 unknown cards, among which are 3 aces. The fraction which expresses the probability of you as dealer receiving an ace as your first up card is 3/44. The fraction which expresses the probability of your not pairing your "ace in the hole" is 41/44; odds against pairing being 41 to 3 or about 14 to 1. Between the first and last players we find quite a range in the various chance problems that present themselves and this fact is mentioned because it has a vital bearing on the successful playing of the game.

The component parts of the fractions of probability are subject to important changes at each turn of a card. As dealer faces successive cards, the denominator, 51, decreases by 1 for each card faced; the numerator decreases only if the desired card is faced. The ace was used merely as an example.

The Rules of Stud Poker

In your consideration of the game of stud poker it is important to know the total number of hands in a pack of cards and to be able to figure the odds against receiving any particular hand, pat. In the minds of some players this detail may be of minor importance, but I believe it should be incorporated in any book which purports to be complete.

A symbol used by mathematicians to express the total number of hands of poker in a pack of cards is "52c5" and means the number of combinations of 52 different things taken 5 at a time, interpreted in figures as follows, 52x51x50x49x48, divided by the product obtained by multiplying 1x2x3x4x5. The number 2,598,960 is the result and it is important because it is the denominator of the fraction which represents the chance of any particular kind of a hand.

The following table of distribution shows the major denominations into which the total of 2,598,960 hands is divided and each figure or number of individual hands is the numerator of the fraction representing the chance of that particular hand:

Straight flushes	40
Four of a kind	624
Full houses	3,744
Ordinary flushes	5,108 *excluding 40 str. fl.*
Ordinary straights	10,200
Three of a kind	54,912
Two pairs	123,552
One pair	1,098,240
No pair	1,302,540
Total number of hands	2,598,960

27

The fewer the number of hands in a denomination, the greater its relative value.

A straight flush, i.e. 5 cards of a suit in sequence.

Four of a kind, i.e. such as 4 nines and any other card.

Full houses, i.e. 3 fours and a pair of tens.

Ordinary flushes, i.e. all five cards of the same suit.

Ordinary straights, i.e. 5 cards in sequence, not of the same suit.

Three of a kind, i.e. 3 kings, 2 cards of different value each.

Two pairs, i.e. 1 pair of sevens, 1 pair of jacks, 1 off card.

One pair, i.e. 1 pair of aces, 3 cards of different value each.

No pair, i.e. no two cards alike, no flush, no sequence.

(Cards of any other denomination may be substituted for the ones mentioned above; they were used merely as an example.)

All suits have the same value in poker.

In an earlier page I said that "the chances are expressed by the fraction of this probability, the denominator being the total number of events possible and the numerator the number of events, favorable;" therefore:

the probability of receiving a straight flush, pat, is expressed by the fraction 40 /2598960; 2,598,920 to 40 or 64,973 to 1 against;

the probability of receiving four of a kind, pat, is expressed by the fraction 624 /2598960; 2,598,336 to 624 or 4,164 to 1 against;

the probability of receiving a full house, pat, is expressed by the fraction 3744 /2598960; 2,595,215 to 3,744 or 693 to 1 against;

the probability of receiving an ordinary flush, pat, is expressed by the fraction 5108 /2598960; 2,593,852 to 5,108 or 508 to 1 against;

the probability of receiving an ordinary straight, pat, is expressed by the fraction 10200/2598960; 2,588,760 to 10,200 or 254 to 1 against;

the probability of receiving three of a kind, pat, is expressed by the fraction 54912/2598960; 2,544,048 to 54,912 or 46 to 1 against;

the probability of receiving two pairs, pat, is expressed by the fraction 123,552/2598960; 2475408 to 123,552 or 20 to 1 against;

the probability of receiving one pair, pat, is expressed by the fraction 1098240/2598960; 1,500,720 to 1,098,240 or 1.37 to 1 against;

hands containing merely "high card" 1302540/2598960; or just about ½, which verifies the fraction used in a following chapter showing the danger attached to increase in the number of players staying to draw or play against the bettor.

These odds represent the chances against receiving any particular hand pat and do not prevail as the deal progresses, so in succeeding pages the method to be used in computing the chances of certain hands, which in individual cases are most likely to be ultimately dealt, will be fully explained. The great difference between the fractions of probability is due to the fact that pat hands of any denomination are based on the ratio of the actual number of hands of that class to the possibilities; viewing the pack as a whole; while, in figuring the chance of a particular hand during the progress of the deal, the calculations are pitched on an entirely different plane. In other words, the collective frequency with which all hands are supposed to occur based on their actual number in the pack is taken into account in calculating the chances of pat hands, whereas after the deal has started and the cards are faced, successively, only that hand or those hands are considered that are actually in process of being made.

The dealer, in dealing the various cards to the several players must distinctly announce the value of each card as it is exposed and call the possibilities of the different hands as the deal progresses.

It so happens that the dealer is and should be held responsible for the orderly dealing of the cards as he is the one who has control of the pack. Before the game starts a rule should be made exacting a forfeit for flagrant violations of the etiquette regarding misdeals.

Every reasonable effort should be made by the dealer to see that all checking, betting, calling, raising or passing has been consummated on any particular round before attempting to deal the cards again. There are also concurrent obligations on the part of each player in the game: he must protect his own hand, conceal his hole card from his opponents, he must not accept more or less cards than the regulation number and should immediately call the dealer's attention to any infraction of rules.

The game is much more interesting if conducted along sound lines and such errors as exposing a hole card inadvertently, dealing exposed cards before betting on a particular round has stopped, dealing too many exposed cards, omitting any player in a deal, having a card faced in pack, exposing the bottom card or failing to have pack cut before dealing can to a great extent be practically eliminated if all players concentrate on the game.

The betting limit must be established before the game starts and in most cases is progressive, a smaller limit on the second and third cards with the permission of a larger bet on the fourth and fifth ones. In most games the limit is also increased when a pair shows on the table, the holder of this pair being given the privilege of making a larger bet than ordinarily could be made.

The player with the highest card showing on the first round must bet and may offer any amount within the limit. On subsequent rounds a player who has first say, or highest cards showing may bet or check but if a bet is offered by any player in proper turn, this bet must be called or raised within the limit by all players desiring to remain in pool.

Ante—the original stake for which you play. Put up before each deal by dealer or all players agreed upon. Like the betting limit, it is so individual that no set rules can be formulated. The amount of the ante and the number of players contributing depend upon rules established by the players themselves. In some games the compulsory first bet by the high man has superseded the ante, but there is no reason why both cannot be the rule if the players desire.

"Calling" means that the bet of any player has been equalled by some one or all players who have received cards and are still in the game. If all cards are dealt to the several players and all bets equalized, all hands in the game, including hole cards, must be shown on the board face up. A player who calls, or is called, must show his hole card if he has stayed throughout the betting and has been dealt five cards. The caller pays to see his opponent's hole card as well as to have a chance to win the pot. Hole cards cannot be concealed after all cards are dealt and all bets are called.

"Raising" means that, in addition to depositing in the pot an amount equivalent to the previous bet or bets, an increased amount is placed therein, which in turn must be equalled by all players in the game, assuming that they desire to draw other cards for the final showdown.

"Passing" or refusing to back your hand with a bet may be done at any time unless a player holds the highest card showing on the first round; after the first round, however, any player may pass whenever he feels that his cards are no longer worth supporting.

"Checking" means that a bettor desires to transfer his betting privilege to another player. It may be either a defensive or offensive play. A strong hand may be "checked," hoping for a bet from an opponent so that the bet can be raised. Be careful how you bet against a "check!"

After all five cards have been dealt to each player in the game and all bets have been equalled, the hands remaining in the pool are exposed for the showdown, the highest hand winning the pot. A player, betting in proper order, making a bet that is not called is entitled to take the pot without showing his hole card.

It is a principle in poker that every player should have a "sight for his pile," that is, he is entitled to all chances to win any pot to which he has contributed provided he has not passed out of the betting. To accomplish this end, the "short show down" has been practically universally accepted. It means that a player who has exhausted his chips, either in betting, calling or raising may continue to draw cards and still have a chance to win that portion of the pot in which he has had a share in building, even though conditions justify the other players in the game making subsequent bets.

In order that this player may win that portion of chips set aside as a result of his inability to continue betting, his hand must be best of all hands in the final show down. He only wins those chips that have been separated, the next highest hand wins the balance of the pool.

Chips once placed in the pot and the owner's hand withdrawn cannot be removed by anyone except the winner of the pool. Talk means nothing in poker, a player may use words to conceal his meaning as well as to express it. The bet's the thing.

If, before betting has stopped on any round, the dealer exposes a card or cards prematurely, a forfeit should be exacted, the amount of the forfeit being agreed on before the game starts and the forfeit being placed in the pot. The card or cards shown must not be given to any player or players but should be reshuffled with the cards remaining in the deck and then dealt to the several players. This rule should work no hardship on any individual over a period of time. The law of averages has a tendency to even up honest mistakes; a player may be deprived of an ace one time and a deuce later on. Accept such situations in a fair-minded manner and your enjoyment of the game will not be impaired.

If a player's hole card is exposed by dealer or any player other than himself, he may play it as his first exposed card and should be entitled to a card on the next deal, faced down.

"Table Stakes" denotes that the betting limit is established by the amount of chips that a player has on the table before him at the time his bet is made. It cannot be increased during the progress of a deal. Additions to one's stakes must be made before betting starts or after it is finished on any particular deal.

No play out of turn can deprive any contestant of his legitimate rights. All players have the fundamental privilege of demanding orderly conduct and procedure in the game and are entitled to all protection of the rules. When an error is made by the dealer that has a tendency to deprive a player of the card that belongs to him at that particular time, the mistake should be corrected as soon as noticed and the card or cards "backed up" so that each player will receive the card that he would have received had no mistake been made.

In case of ties the hand holding highest card or cards is awarded the pot, if the hands remaining in the game are tied throughout, then the pot is divided equally.

After the deal has started there should be no further "cutting" of the deck except in case of mis-deal. No player has the right to demand a new shuffle or cut for frivolous reasons.

"There are no mis-deals in poker." No doubt any one who has played "stud" over a period of time has heard this statement quite often; however, it is merely arbitrary and has no basis in fact.

In order to expedite the game and nullify the efforts of players who might deliberately do those things that would call for a mis-deal with the subsequent re-shuffling and re-dealing of the cards, it is in the interest of stud that a mis-deal be declared only when those things are done that would have a tendency to influence betting by giving a player certain information that would be denied him in the orderly procedure of the deal.

No player is entitled to any information in the game of stud poker gratuitously except that which might be common to all; he must earn any advantage through obedience to the rules and observance of betting principles. Previous to betting, he should have no knowledge stronger than faith regarding the value of the card or cards that he will be dealt in a game.

To admit any great number of excuses for mis-deals would, to a great extent, encourage the practice; therefore, assuming the proper shuffling and "cutting" of the deck before the play begins, the only reason for mis-deals are as follows:

Exposing bottom card in pack;

A card faced in pack;

Dealing too many exposed cards;

Dealing of exposed cards prematurely.

These four errors are fundamental, they give a player who has not bet certain information that no doubt influences his betting. As soon as any one of the four mistakes is discovered, the exposed card or cards should be immediately replaced in the stock and the pack shuffled and cut before resuming the deal.

The Mechanics of Stud Poker

Stud poker is a game of psychological inferences as well as mathematical exactness. Any number of players, from three to ten can play it. A number in excess of ten renders the game too unwieldly and less than three is obviously too small. It is the author's opinion that seven or eight players make the ideal game. Eight players, including dealer, are used in all calculations in this book, except as noted, but the reader can make his own deductions, using the number of players in his mental arithmetic consistent with the occasion confronting him.

A full pack of fifty-two cards should be used, as a number in excess or insufficient renders calculations more or less inaccurate. Anyone may deal, dealer being chosen by any method which the players agree upon; one of the players usually picks up the pack, shuffles it, deals the cards around face up, one to each player, the first player receiving a jack being the one to start the game as dealer. After the dealer is designated, he assembles all the cards, shuffles them, cuts the pack if he so desires and presents it to the player on his right for cutting. In this connection, the dealer should always cut the pack before presenting it to the player on his right, as this player may elect not to cut. If the dealer has shuffled the pack with the cards facing away from himself, there is strong probability that the other players may know what card is on the bottom; if the dealer handles the pack with the cards facing himself, he probably knows what is on the bottom to the exclusion of the other players, so to eliminate any post-mortems relative to the dealer's fairness, always see that the cards are cut at least once after shuffling. Failure to "cut" the pack is a mis-deal.

After the pack has been properly shuffled and "cut," the dealer, beginning with player on his immediate left, deals each one a card, faced down, himself last. He then deals each player a card face up, as before. The player with the highest card showing must, of necessity, bet first. The player on the bettor's immediate left must do one of the following three things: call the bet by placing in the pot an equivalent value in chips; pass, which means that he turns his hand down and does not play any more until some player wins the present pot and a new deal is started; or raise within the limit, which means that he not only calls the first bettor by depositing the same amount of chips in the pot but makes any additional bet which other players, including original bettor, must equal in their proper turn.

Each player, in proper order, has the privilege of betting, calling or raising as he sees fit and can also pass or check unless he is "high man" after the first faced up card is dealt. A player who is high, faced up, on deals after the first round does not have to bet unless he desires to do so; he may "check" the betting, but he must at least place in the pot on any particular round an amount of chips equal to any bets made on this round if he elects to stay in for the final call or showdown. Five cards, four faced up, and the first one down, or "in the hole," are dealt in stud poker and betting starts as soon as the first round of faced up cards is distributed.

As soon as all players are served, including dealer, who is served last, betting begins, and ends for the round after all players have had their say. The cards are then dealt around again to all the players remaining in the game. The player with the highest hand showing, after each deal, always has the right to bet

36

first if he desires to do so. Other players may pass, call or raise as before. A player who drops out of the game at any time before the fifth card is dealt does not have to show his hole card. All players who remain in the game until the fifth or final card is dealt and who call the bet of the player making the last wager must show all their cards, including hole card in the final showdown. Any player who has called the last bet must show all of his cards, face up; he cannot conceal his hole card and admit defeat. This rule is salutary as, to a great extent, it prohibits collusion.

The crucial moment in stud poker occurs just as soon as a player receives his first card, faced up. This card is the second one he is dealt, the first one being faced down, or "in the hole." Right here is where your poker ingenuity should make itself known as your knowledge of how to play your hole card will either make or mar your game.

Successful poker is based on the theory that no hand should be played unless the hole card is as high or higher than any card showing in an opponent's hand; this idea should be kept in mind constantly, even thought a player for one reason or another deviates from the precept at times. Of course, if you are high, showing on the first round, you are obliged to bet regardless of the value of your hole card.

The idea of insisting that your hole card, paired, must be able to beat any exposed card in an opponent's hand if this card were paired, is the fundamental principle of the game and is so basic that it hardly seems necessary to repeat it, but "repetition makes reputation." It is "the secret of the philosopher's stone."

Do not wait until the third or fourth card is dealt before "taking stock" to see just what the possibilities are. A player who does this frequently finds himself "out on a limb." Play your hole card; this is the card that you should want to pair. It does not avail you anything to pair a card that is faced up in your hand in comparison to the advantage to be gained in the pairing of the card "in the hole," assuming of course that the hole card has real value. To win "second money" in stud is an empty honor. If you pair a card, showing, in your hand and opponents continue to stay, that is a bad sign, if you believe in signs, so, "shorten sail and stand by for a squall." If opponents drop out of the game, you win very little.

Right here, however, is the place for the author and the reader to understand each other. Just because, as a matter of principle, I say always turn your hand down under certain conditions which I have explained, do not take the advice too literally. There may be times and circumstances when you would want to play a hand out, just to see or understand some or all of your opponents' playing strategy. For instance, you may desire to see what value a player attaches to his hole card. Does he come in with treys or fours or fives "in the hole?" It may be worth a few pots in the early stages of the game to secure this knowledge, because "knowledge is power" if properly used. Also, the odds in the betting may be tempting, justifying a call.

Being in the game and calling the bets as they are made gives you certain privileges that you may not feel like taking if you had dropped out of the betting. As an example, without making yourself disagreeable, you can demand that all players come into the pot in proper turn, you can insist that the deal proceed in an orderly manner, you can demand that the final showdown be done "according to Hoyle," and last but not least, you will probably not antagonize the other players so much by insisting on the rules when you are in the game as you would under other circumstances.

There is also a thrill attached to outdrawing a player who undoubtedly has you beaten at the start.

You won't enjoy this thrill very often, but it does occur once in a while.

To stick to one, hard and fast rule precludes the possibility of occasionally venturing in pots that offer a good return on the investment. It sort of stereotypes a player, and this is bad for the stud addict. His style of play becomes known and he seldom wins any large pots as other players have him marked.

Do not try to outdraw a player who has indicated strength unless the odds in the pot and chance of improvement at the time you bet justify the attempt. In a case like this, the relative positions of all players should be taken into consideration before deciding what to do. If the bettor has his bet called by several players before the play reaches you, it is well to try to analyze the play of the callers possibly more carefully than you do the bettor's. The original bettor may be bluffing, the callers are more apt to be telling the truth. It is almost a certainty that one or more of the callers have hands of importance or they would not be calling the bet.

Never make any vulgar display of power, always remember that it does not add to your stature as a poker player to be dealt three aces in a game. The same thing could happen to a three-year-old child. The difference between the tycoon and the tyro is in the manner in which the cards are played.

Except for an occasional publicity or advertising purpose, never display your hole card unless you are called. When you show your hole card it tells your opponents something and to tell an opponent anything in stud poker, except possibly, "I've got 'em pal," is dangerous. Let your opponent find out for himself through the mechanics of the game, what you have studied and learned about the greatest game of them all. Action in stud is fast, the known cards destroy the deck's symmetry and the players are continually dropping out, so try to evaluate your hand and its potentialities as promptly as possible. Do not wait until it is too late!

In this discussion of stud poker no thought has been given to "wild" cards, or freakish hands, but, in view of the widespread custom, I believe some comment is necessary.

In order that the "old line" player's ability may be somewhat lessened and the novice be given greater chance to win, certain cards, in most cases deuces, are sometimes designated "wild." This means that deuces or any card called "wild" take the value that the holder desires.

A pair of sixes and a deuce may be played as three sixes; the "wild" card can also be used as a "filler" to complete a straight or flush. Two pairs and a "wild" card may be played as a full house. Four hearts in sequence and a "wild" card may be termed a straight flush. When any card or cards have been named as "wild" nearly all calculations are, to a great extent, nullified but, even so, the student of the game has a distinct advantage over the player who does not study its fundamentals.

While playing a game with some cards "wild" increases the excitement it does not always result in a concurrent increase in knowledge of the game's basic principles; for this reason it would be wise for anyone desiring to learn how to play winning stud to forsake the momentary pleasure of "deuces loose" in favor of that more enduring quality, namely, that of learning how to play the cards at their true values.

With "wild" cards, the tendency is to discount the good player's ability rather than to add strength to the beginner's efforts. The true seeker of "the more abundant life" in the world of cards will try to emulate the example of those who have learned how to play stud poker properly, instead of insisting that this ability be forsaken in order that some player or players may possibly profit thereby.

Cards are played at their face value and to miscall your hand does not prevent your winning the pot in the showdown if your hand is actually best of all hands in the final call. When "wild" cards are played however, the hand is played at the value that the holder declares, assuming that the cards will support the valuation. A player may call his hand as an "ace full" and display three aces, four and a deuce, deuces being wild." He actually has four aces but is beaten by four sixes. Be careful in the evaluation of a hand containing "wild" cards in order that you may not receive a self-imposed penalty. In cases of ties, natural cards beat fillers. A hand containing two aces and a deuce beats one containing two deuces and an ace. Think of the order of strength of the hands and always value the hand at its greatest worth.

In the category of freakish hands is that perennial favorite known as "high and low." This is a form of poker in which the pot is divided evenly between the holders of the highest and lowest hands after the final showdown. It serves as an "interest holder," keeping everybody in the game and at the same time permits a distribution of the total stakes involved along lines that oftentimes are amusing in the extreme.

Even though you may be a splendid poker player under normal conditions, in this game you will often find that in the showdown you divide the pot with some opponent who plays the game as though he had never heard of it before.

I do not care to go on record as saying that it is impossible to consider this form of stud in any serious manner as sometime, somewhere or somehow, someone may formulate a system that might impeach my theory, but, "pending the arrival of the millennium," I will venture the assertion that probably the sole redeeming feature of "high and low" and other variations of stud is that they are equally fair to all.

When "wild" cards are being played, it is possible to hold "five of a kind." This is the highest hand that can be held and beats all others.

When you consider the cohesiveness of the different forms of the game of poker you will realize the necessity of becoming well informed in its fundamentals so that regardless of the particular names by which these ramifications are called you will understand they all have certain underlying principles which, to a great extent, remain unchanged. Just remember that the more open the game or the greater the number of "wild" cards, the higher should be the minimum value of the hand that you concede chance to win.

As a final comment on the subject of wild cards and other varieties of the game, it may be said that knowledge of the game should not be assassinated as though it were a hostile witness, and that is just what the playing of these hands has a tendency to do.

The Mathematics of Stud Poker

1. What are the probabilities of deuces, backed, being beaten by additions to the number of players who stay to draw against them?

2. What are the probabilities of aces, backed, being beaten by additions to the number of players who stay to draw against them?

3. What is the probability of improvement by player who has pair, backed?

4. What is the probability of either ace, or king, backed, being paired by the dealing of the three remaining cards?

5. What is the probability of ace or king being held in hole by some one of seven opponents after the first "up" card is dealt, provided none on table showing and you have neither in hole?

6. Suppose an opponent has given strong evidence of having treys, backed; you have an ace "in the hole"; what are the relative chances or probabilities of your pairing your ace, vs. your opponent's improving his treys?

7. Suppose an opponent has given strong evidence of having queens, backed; you have ace, king, backed; what are the relative chances of your pairing either vs. your opponent's chances of improving his queens?

8. In a game of stud poker after dealing one card around, "in the hole" and one card around, face up; one player has a king showing, what are the odds against this player having a king, also, "in the hole"?

9. At the end of a five card deal, you have two pairs, one of your opponents has a 4 straight, showing. What are the odds against his hand being filled?

10. At the end of a five card deal, you have a straight, one of your opponents has a 4 flush, showing. What are the odds against his having a flush?

11. At the end of a five card deal, you have a flush, one of your opponents has two pairs, showing. What are the odds against his having a full house?

12. At the end of a five card deal, you hold a full house, one of your opponents has 3 tens showing. What are the odds against his having the 4th ten in the hole?

13. At the end of a five card deal, you have 4 treys, one of your opponents has a 4 straight flush showing. What are the odds against his hand being made?

14. Suppose you are the first player to be dealt cards in a stud game, the player on the dealer's immediate left. What are the odds against your naming, in advance, the pair that you are to be dealt, back to back?

15. Are the odds the same against cutting two kings, consecutively, from one pack of cards, and two kings, consecutively from two packs?

16. What are the odds against drawing a "face" card from a full pack in one draw? Two draws? Three draws?

Correct answers to these questions will be found in this chapter.

As the writer sees the game of stud, the proper time to appraise the various hands in the game is immediately after every player has received his first card, faced up, the second card dealt. If your hole card is not as high or higher than the highest card showing in an opponent's hand, throw your cards in the discard. If your card, showing, is the highest you must bet first, the other players passing, calling or raising in proper order.

Make your decision as soon as you see the other cards on the table, always playing in your correct turn. Do not be misled by the fact that there are three more cards to be dealt you from which you hope to be able to pair one or other of your first two cards. All the other players in the game have the same chance, so the odds are certainly against you from the start, if you are low. If you can improve your hand, so can your opponent; if he improves, he probably can beat any improvement that you may make, also.

Stud poker is entitled to more than a casual examination if it is to be enjoyed to its fullest extent. The mathematics of the game can be readily appreciated if the devotee will give just a little thought to its fundamentals. The laws of percentage relating to the chances of making certain hands are so well defined that only a person ignorant of card playing would say that they are inoperative. The game is most amenable to sound mathematical deduction and even in comparison with that present holder of public affection, bridge, stud loses nothing but emerges more glorious than ever.

No man of even ordinary intelligence would say that every individual stud poker game is purely a question of arithmetic, 100%. I am willing to admit that what is commonly called "luck" does enter the "picture" to a minor extent, but eventually the element of "luck" is almost completely obliterated and the consistent winners are the ones whose knowledge of the laws of chance and probability governing the flux and reflux of skillful play is more than nominal.

I have sat in games with persons who apparently had no knowledge of the mathematics of the game. I have seen them win, too, but over a period of time and not an immeasurable period either, these players almost invariably lose. Their losses are just about in direct proportion to the game's limits.

Should one's poker playing principles be based on a "lying and lying in wait" policy, or should the game be played aggressively, when good cards are held?

This is a problem that has agitated and will continue to upset the minds of poker players for all time, no doubt. It is one that each individual desires to decide for himself; however, I would like to present a few reasons why, when good cards are held, an aggressive style of play, over a period of time, is more likely to prove the better strategy. To bet or not to bet, that is the question. To bet is positive, active; not to bet is negative, passive. In the following table I have tried to illustrate the two extremes and at the same time, justify my reasons for "taking up the cudgel" in behalf of aggressiveness in playing stud, when you have a good hand.

Bet.

If win; will get larger return because high card is justified in betting. Not every player will concede you a pair, backed.

If lose, through being outdrawn; this will not happen often enough to offset your increased winnings by generally maintaining this style of play.

No Bet.

If win; pots will be smaller as other players will be let in cheaply. To expect opponents to assume the offensive, except in occasional cases, is too negative in action to produce satisfactory results.

If lose; the ill results are mostly psychological, a mental hazard; if you lose holding good cards, would your chance of winning increase with bad ones? A bet, eliminating some competition, no doubt would have changed the outcome.

In any discussion regarding the relative merits of the two systems, it would be silly to contend that aggressive playing when good cards are held "types" a player to a greater degree than would the opposite style of play; that other players, soon discerning this line of offense would be governed accordingly. Most

46

assuredly, staying in a pot, merely calling, in the face of bets, calls and raises, would certainly indicate just as much power and really should mean the presence of a stronger hand than if the player had made the first bet. A first bettor may be bluffing; callers, by various inferences, should at least have something on which to call.

The main idea and the most successful one in stud poker is to cultivate "a change of pace." Always avoid mannerisms that may have a tendency to "telegraph" your hand's value to smart players, try to keep them guessing. One hard, set and fast rule, without any deviation, is not likely to produce the best results; however, it is very easy to illustrate the fallacy of not betting, so as to eliminate competition when a small pair, deuces, for example, is held back to back, this pair no doubt being the best hand on the table at the particular moment; the odds against receiving a pair, back to back, being, as we have seen, approximately 16 to 1.

The following example, quoted from Proctor, is used with the permission of the Fitzgerald Publishing Corporation. To me, it seems to be quite appropriate at this time and certainly adds strength to similar convictions regarding the game of stud poker.

"Many, even among gamblers, know so little of the theory of probability in its relation to additions to the number of players who stay to play against the bettor that it might not be wrong at this time to comment on the subject. The effect of increase in the number of other contestants can readily be measured and is easily illustrated.

"For example—supposing a player casts a die against only one opponent and this player casts four; the odds are in favor of his not being beaten, as there are only two casts which will beat him and four which will not. The fraction which expresses the probability of his not being beaten is 2/3.

"If there now comes an additional opponent, his

chance of not beating the first player's roll of four is also 2/3. The chance that neither will throw better than four is obtained by multiplying 2/3x2/3, or 4/9; the chance that either one or the other or both opponents will beat the first player's cast of four is 5/9 or odds of 5 to 4 against the original caster.

"Suppose a third opponent now comes into the game, his individual chance of not beating the first thrower is likewise 2/3 but the combined chances of the first player's cast of four not being beaten is found by multiplying 2/3x2/3x2/3, or 8/27; chance of being beaten is 19/27 (notice that the sum of these two fractions is unity) or odds of 19 to 8 in favor of original caster being beaten and with every increase in the number of opponents the chance of the original player's cast of four being beaten is greatly augmented. With only one opponent, the odds in the original caster's favor are 2 to 1; with three opponents the odds are 19 to 8 against him."

The fractions illustrative of chance and probability in various deals of stud poker are just as sound, fundamentally, and can be made subject matter of highly interesting speculation.

[The tables in this chapter show the probabilities of deuces, fives, eights, jacks and aces being outdrawn in a five card deal and do not take into account the concurrent probability of improvement by the holders of these backed pairs. In the chapter following, on "netods," this concurrent probability of improvement is considered at length.]

Of the 2,598,960 hands in poker, just about one half of them contain a value of one pair or better, the number being 1,296,420, so the fraction that expresses the probability of receiving a pair or better in a deal of 5 cards is practically 1/2.

Suppose further, that the holder of the deuces, backed, is playing in an 8-hand game and the fraction 1/2 represents the probability of any player receiving a pair or higher in a deal of five cards. There are seven opponents; therefore, the following table shows the probability of a pair or better being held by one or more opponents in an eight hand stud game.

One opponent; chance of no pair or higher, 1/2; chance of pair or higher, 1/2; odds are even.

Two opponents; 1 minus the second power of 1/2; odds in favor, 3 to 1.

Three opponents; 1 minus the third power of 1/2; odds in favor, 7 to 1.

Four opponents; 1 minus the fourth power of 1/2; odds in favor, 15 to 1.

Five opponents; 1 minus the fifth power of 1/2; odds in favor, 31 to 1.

Six opponents; 1 minus the sixth power of 1/2; odds in favor, 63 to 1.

Seven opponents; 1 minus the seventh power of 1/2; odds in favor, 127 to 1.

Furthermore, granted that there is a pair among your opponents, it is most certainly sure to be higher in value than your deuces, or any other small pair that you might possibly have, backed; so if you decide to play your hand at all, play it; and remember that "the gambler bets, the sucker calls."

"The gambler bets, the sucker calls," although a bromide, has a most reasonable explanation. The gambler, or the bettor, has a two-to-one advantage over the sucker, or the caller. There is the chance that his bet will not be called, or if it is called, there is also the chance that in the showdown his cards will be of higher value than the caller's. The caller's only chance is that his cards are actually of higher value than the bettor's.

In so far as the necessity of having a hand justifying the bet is concerned, the bettor is no worse off than the caller; as a matter of fact, he is in a more advantageous position because you do not need a hand as powerful on which to bet as is needed when you call.

Poor cards plus a bet or raise will win oftener than poor cards plus merely a call.

"Cut short your losses; let your profits run on!" Even though you are playing a game in which every player has to ante on every deal, you can still adhere to the principles outlined in this book. When the cards are not "breaking" properly for you in the denomination of the hole cards that you are receiving, do not throw good money after bad. Just because your ante belongs to the pot, do not lose courage or perspective. You will eventually be favored with your share of cards of high value so try to cultivate a compensatory system of betting.

When you win you will win an ante from each and every player in the game and you may rest assured that in so far as the amount of the ante is concerned, you will do better than break even. In addition, you will have an edge on the other players because you will have learned the lesson of self-control.

Suppose we consider another deal of stud poker; eight players. You discover that you have a pair of fives, backed. How does increase in the number of players staying to play against your fives affect the chances of your wining the pot?

It would be reasonable to assume that only a hand containing a pair of sixes or better could offer you any serious opposition; so let's figure the odds against some one of seven opponents ending the five-card deal with a hand of like value.

(There is a total of 1,098,240 single pair hands, equally divided among the 13 denominations; therefore, each denomination contains 84,480 possible pairs.)

Of the 2,598,960 hands in poker, there is a total of 958,500 hands containing a value of a pair of sixes or better. The number 958,500 is obtained as follows; number of hands, of value two pairs or better, 198,180; plus 760,320, the number of one-pair hands, sixes through aces. The fraction 958500/2598960, or in round figures, 1/3, therefore represents the chance of one opponent receiving a hand, of value a pair of sixes or better; the odds against, being 2 to 1.

(The following table shows the probability of a pair of sixes or better, being held by one or more opponents in an eight hand stud game.)

One opponent; chances of sixes or better being held, 1/3; not held, 2/3; odds against equals 2 to 1.

Two opponents; 1 minus the second power of 2/3; odds in favor, 5 to 4.

Three opponents; 1 minus the third power of 2/3; odds in favor, 2 and 3/8 to 1.

Four opponents; 1 minus the fourth power of 2/3; odds in favor, about 4 to 1.

Five opponents; 1 minus the fifth power of 2/3; odds in favor, about 6 and 1/2 to 1.

Six opponents; 1 minus the sixth power of 2/3; odds in favor, about 10 and 1/2 to 1.

Seven opponents; 1 minus the seventh power of 2/3; odds in favor, 16 to 1.

And we can still produce more evidence of the fallacy of "letting them in light" when you hold a good hand, unless you want to express your "rugged individualism"; but, boys! there is a "new deal" all around and here it is in stud!

I suppose that almost every stud poker player would be willing to accept a pair of jacks, backed, and take his chances of being outdrawn, but do not think for one moment that it cannot be done! The number of hands in a pack of cards containing a value of a pair of queens or better is 451,620. It is obtained as follows; number of hands of value, two pairs or better, 198,180; plus 253,440; the number of one-pair hands, queens through aces.

The fraction that expresses the probability of a player receiving a hand, of value queens or better is, therefore, 451620/2598960; in a simpler fraction, 1/6. The odds against, being 5 to 1.

(The following table shows the probability of a pair of queens or better being held by one or more opponents in an eight hand stud game.)

One opponent; chance that queens or better are held, 1/6; not held, 5/6; odds against, 5 to 1.

Two opponents; 1 minus the second power of 5/6; odds against, 2 and 1/4 to 1.

Three opponents; 1 minus the third power of 5/6; odds against, 1 and 3/8 to 1.

Four opponents; 1 minus the fourth power of 5/6; odds in favor, 671 to 625.

Five opponents; 1 minus the fifth power of 5/6; odds in favor, about 1 and 1/2 to 1.

Six opponents; 1 minus the sixth power of 5/6; odds in favor, 2 to 1.

Seven opponents; 1 minus the seventh power of 5/6; odds in favor, 2 and 4/7 to 1.

We have seen what additions to the number of players do to the chances of a player with deuces, fives or jacks, backed, winning a pot, now suppose we take the case of the strongest possible hand at the start, aces, backed. How does the holder of aces fare against increased opposition?

It is begging the question to say that you will let seven, eight or nine players draw against your aces and take your chances of winning. Of course, the probabilities are greatly in favor of a player with this strong hand ultimately gaining the pot, but to admit this does not destroy the force of the argument. Holding aces, you make no effort to protect them by betting as you want plenty of "company."

Of the total hands in the deck, numbering 2,598,960, there are 198,180 containing a value of two pairs or better. The fraction that expresses the probability of a player being dealt a poker hand of value, two pairs or better is, therefore, 198180/2598960 or 1/13. The fraction that expresses the probability that a player will not receive a hand of this value is 12/13. (Two pairs or better are necessary in order to beat aces.)

(The following table shows the probability of two pairs or better being held by one or more opponents in an eight hand stud game.)

One opponent; chance of two pairs or better, 1/13; no two pairs or better, 12/13; odds against, 12 to 1.

Two opponents; 1 minus the second power of 12/13; odds against, 6 to 1.

Three opponents; 1 minus the third power of 12/13; odds against, 3 and 2/3 to 1.

Four opponents; 1 minus the fourth power of 12/13; odds against, 2 and 5/8 to 1.

Five opponents; 1 minus the fifth power of 12/13; odds against, 2 to 1.

Six opponents; 1 minus the sixth power of 12/13; odds against, 1 and 1/2 to 1.

Seven opponents; 1 minus the seventh power of 12/13; odds against, 1 and 1/3 to 1.

While the examples quoted are of course a priori and do not take into account the chance of improvement by a player holding a backed pair, yet they tell a story of their own and are certainly indicative of something; they probably clarify some ideas about stud poker which heretofore have been merely vague and indistinct in the minds of poker players.

Suppose for example, a player with a very high pair, back to back, does not bet his hand, let's see what might happen to the pot, ultimately. If he does not bet, thereby permitting an increased number of opponents to draw cards against him, he runs a chance of losing the pot because of the additional number of players. If he does not bet yet wins the pot he does not win nearly as much money as his hand would entitle him to receive as his lack of aggressiveness has made the playing inexpensive for his adversaries.

If he does bet, with an ace or king, for instance, as his first "up" card, he should at least receive a respec-

table number of calls as the high card is always justified in "stepping out." We have seen that the odds
against getting a pair back to back are about 16 to 1,
so not every player would give him credit for the high
hand.

Whether he bets or not, of course, he can still be
outdrawn, but if he bets it will not happen as often
because his chances of being beaten are increased by
additions to the number of players who stay to draw
against him and continued betting tends to diminish
this opposition. If his betting does not decrease the
number of his opponents, he probably can "stand the
gaff" as well as they. If he wins, which most likely
he will, he need have no regrets because he has charged
"all the traffic will bear." If he loses, even though he
has bet his hand as he should have done, he need have
no misgivings because by not betting and permitting
increased opposition would have insured his defeat to
a greater degree. The old adage, "Fortune favors the
brave," certainly applies in poker.

Boys! when you have a good hand, make your
opponents pay to see it; when, in your opinion, your
hand is no good, do not let curiosity about the other
fellow's hand get the better of you. Do not "sit" on
them, play them! Being outdrawn because of the lack
of protection that you give your hand makes most of
these "Talkative Thomases, Muttering Michaels and
Chattering Charleys." And do not show your hole card
unless you are called! "Equity follows the law," in cards
as well as elsewhere.

I said in a previous page that the proper time to
appraise your hand is immediately after you receive
your first "up" card, the second card dealt. Throw
your hand in the discard if your hole card is not as
high or higher than the highest card showing in an
opponent's hand. If you let this norm be your guiding
star you will find that it is a good rule. Also, remember
that your opponent with his higher card has better

than an "even break." Due regard, of course, must be given to the odds in the pot at the time a bet is made or contemplated and the chance of improvement must be figured as closely as possible. If an opponent has you beaten in sight there is a possibility that you are "doubly" beaten, taking his hole card into consideration.

In stud poker the idea is not only to be able to beat any single opponent in the final showdown but to be able to beat all opponents after the fifth card is dealt. To have second best hand is not at all consoling, as there is an infinite difference between the hand that wins and the hand that loses. If you are really "sold" on the idea that a player has either a pair of aces or merely "ace high" isn't it just as logical to call with deuces as with kings? Barring the probability of an opponent having a pair somewhere between aces and "ace high," if he has aces, your kings are no good, if he does not have aces, then your deuces are good. Why not give the subject some thought?

Although the chances of being dealt a pair back to back are the same irrespective of denomination, aces and deuces represent the extremes in value of single pairs which a player might receive in a deal of stud poker. Hoving considered the extremes in our previous calculations, suppose we take a pair that represents the mean, so we will have a mathematical picture more nearly complete of the danger to the holder attached to increase in the number of players who stay to play against a pair, backed.

Suppose, for example, you are playing in an eight-hand game and you receive a pair of eights, backed, eights being a happy medium. there being six pairs above and six below, in value.

When you consider that the odds against improvement of a pair, backed, are about 3 to 1, it means that you must play your smaller pairs for all they are worth in the early stages of the game as the subsequent dealing of the three remaining cards is of more value to the weaker hands than it is to the stronger ones; it being another principle of poker that the stronger the hand is at the start, the harder it is to improve. This principle applies to draw poker, as well. The draw always being of more value to a weak hand than it is to a strong one.

Of the 2,598,960 hands in poker, 52c5, (this symbol being explained in the rules), there is a total of 705,060 hands containing a value of a pair of nines or better. The number 705,060 is obtained as follows; number of hands in pack, value, two pairs or better, 198,180; plus 506,880, the number of hands, of value, one pair, nines through aces. The fraction that expresses the probability that a player will receive a hand in stud poker, of value, a pair of nines or better is, therefore, 705060/2598960. In round figures, approximately 1/4; that he will not, 3/4; odds against, being 3 to 1. Let's see how the odds change as the number of players increases.

(The following table shows the probability of a pair of nines or better being held by one or more opponents in an eight hand stud game.)

One opponent; chance that nines or better are held, 1/4; not held, 3/4; odds against, 3 to 1.

Two opponents; 1 minus the second power of 3/4; odds against, 9 to 7.

Three opponents; 1 minus the third power of 3/4; odds in favor, 1 and 1/3 to 1.

Four opponents; 1 minus the fourth power of 3/4; odds in favor, about 2 to 1.

Five opponents; 1 minus the fifth power of 3/4; odds in favor, about 3 to 1.

Six opponents; 1 minus the sixth power of 3/4; odds in favor, 4 and 3/5 to 1.

Seven opponents; 1 minus the seventh power of 3/4; odds in favor, about 6 and 1/2 to 1.

Do not let anyone tell you that an observance of the principles found in this book is what is known as "cut throat" poker as every stud player worthy of his "salt" will endeavor to play that style of poker which, in his opinion, is best calculated to permit him to win. That he desires to win through honest methods goes without saying, but he should also have competitive spirit and knowledge of proper play if the game is to be thoroughly enjoyed.

With the examples of the deuces, fives, aces, jacks and eights fresh in our minds it might not be amiss at this moment to consider a few rules of precepts that might possibly clarify the game's procedure and at the same time assist us in our effort to understand stud poker more thoroughly. They are as follows:

Play your hole card, discard your hand unless your hole card is as high or higher than any card showing, in any opponents' hand (unless you have to bet, first, with highest exposed card), bear in mind that the known cards destroy the symmetry of the deck and that the calculus of probability changes with the rapidity of a motion picture film as the cards are faced on the table, observe the reactions of the various players as their cards are dealt and you will travel a long way on the road to mastery of the game.

THE "RULE OF NINETEEN"

In fixing the minimum value of the first two cards in stud, that they consider worthwhile, some players are guided by the "rule of nineteen." This idea is based on the principle that the value of the first two cards must total at least 19, allowing a value of 10 for every card from the ten spot through the ace, also taking in the nines.

This rule, while good, is not advocated generally because it lacks flexibility.

The idea of requiring the value of your hole card to be as high or higher than any card showing among your opponents seems, to me, to possess all attributes necessary for a successful stay in stud poker. This rule is not nearly as rigid as the "rule of nineteen."

The "rule of nineteen" gives your opponents too much opportunity to appraise your hand independently of the other hands in the game. Too strict an adherence to it makes your hands easy to read.

The hole card norm, as we might call it, forces your opponents to measure your probable hole card against all cards showing and requires more time and effort on their part.

In order to simplify my calculations and to make the mathematics more easily understood, I used the fractions, 1/2, 1/3, 1/4, 1/6 and 1/13, respectively, as being illustrative of the probabilities of deuces, fives, eights, jacks and aces being outdrawn by an individual opponent.

The fractions, 1/2 and 1/13, for deuces and aces are extremely close. The fractions, 1/3, 1/4 and 1/6, for fives, eights and jacks are not quite as accurate but they are close enough to be used without fear of being considered incorrect. Even though arbitrary, using the fractions 1/3, 1/4 and 1/6 will not seriously affect conclusions in regard to correct play, as the abstract, overall probabilities are not unreasonably distorted. All of these fractions have one thing in common, the numerator of each is "one," giving a sort of uniformity to the extensions and at the same time holding the products down to a mimimum.

The reader will note that in the examples used, showing the probabilities of certain pairs, backed, being outdrawn, I have shown the results of seven opponents staying to draw all five cards against the holders of the pairs.

The progression is set forth in a manner that will permit the reader to see instantly the result of any number of opponents, from one through seven, playing against a pair, backed, but obviously does not take into account situations where two or three opponents draw only three or four cards, then drop out of the game, leaving four or five players to continue drawing cards, against the holder of the pair, until the fifth card is dealt.

The fractions of probability used, namely, 1/2, 1/3, 1/4, 1/6 and 1/13, are all based on the homogeneity of the deck. They obtain only when the deck is viewed in the light of the symmetricality of its whole and are concerned solely with the unknown. As soon as the dealer starts facing the cards upward, the fractions of probability begin to change, and, as stated in a preceding page, the denominator decreases one for every card faced, the numerator decreasing only when the desired card is exposed.

The intelligent way to make use of information of this kind, naturally, is away from the stud table. The chance problems that can be evolved are so numerous that it would be impossible to portray any great number of them in an article of such limited scope as the present one.

We must also remember that even though a hand has real, positive value in itself, yet relatively, it may have no value at all in the final showdown. Just as "in the country of the blind, the one-eyed man is King," so, also in stud, it's the relative, not actual value of hands that counts. This is the real charm of stud poker and is the unknown element that makes it worth while.

The law of diminishing returns holds as well in stud as it does in economics. While no one is unmindful of the sense of personal security afforded by a superlative hand, it is a fact that very strong hands, such as two pairs, threes, straights, flushes and full houses will not win nearly so much in proportion to their scarcity and intrinsic worth as will a single high pair, assuming that the pair is not showing.

Of course, we cannot regulate the fall of the cards

in stud poker; they must be played as dealt but when you consider that of the 2,598,960 hands in the game, only 198,180 are of value, two pairs or better, it behooves us to learn how to play single pairs properly and merely take hands of higher value in stride. Take care of the single pairs, hands of higher value will take care of themselves.

It being an established principle in poker that the greater the number of players, the higher your hand in value should be in order that you concede it chance to win, a conservative player may desire arbitrarily to exclude his hand from participation at any time that he does not have at least an ace or king "in the hole." A desire to throw extra precaution around his poker playing might dictate to him that not only should his hole card be as high or higher than that of any opponent's showing, but that his hole card should be at least a king.

Let us suppose an eight-hand game of stud in which you, as dealer, receive a queen in the hole. Your first card up is a nine. One of your opponents has a jack showing. The jack, being the highest card in sight, bets and is called by all subsequent players up to you, one bet and six callers. The question for you to decide is, "Does my queen in the hole justify my calling?"

Since there are no artificial reasons why mathematical calculations should not govern the play of the cards in stud poker, let us consider the chance or probability of some one of seven opponents having either an ace or king in the hole, there being none showing on the table.

In an eight-hand game of stud, after the first "up" cards are dealt, nine cards are revealed, eight showing on the board and your own hole card. Among the 43 unknown cards are 4 aces and 4 kings. The fraction that expresses the probability of one opponent having either ace or king in the hole is 8/43, or 1/5 in round figures. The fraction 4/5 expresses the probability that one opponent does not have an ace or king in the hole.

Now proceed with the calculations:

One opponent; chance of ace or king in hole, 1/5; chance of no ace or king, 4/5; odds against one opponent having either ace or king in hole, 4 to 1.

Two opponents; 1 minus the second power of 4/5; odds against, about 2 to 1.

Three opponents; 1 minus the third power of 4/5; odds are about even.

Four opponents; 1 minus the fourth power of 4/5; odds in favor, about 1 and 1/2 to 1.

Five opponents; 1 minus the fifth power of 4/5; odds in favor, 2 to 1.

Six opponents; 1 minus the sixth power of 4/5; odds in favor, about 3 to 1.

Seven opponents; 1 minus the seventh power of 4/5; odds in favor, about 4 to 1.

It would seem from the foregoing that your queen in the hole would merely get you in trouble if you called. Everybody has the same chance in stud poker and it is just as easy for your opponent to pair his higher hole card as it is for you to pair your lower one. Your style of play must be adjusted to suit the occasion but study the basic ideas of stud and do not be swayed by apparent probabilities that are merely vague and indistinct.

In stud poker, by appraising the hands just as soon as the first "up" card is dealt and observing the reactions of the several players as they receive their cards, you are placed in a better position to judge the ultimate value of your own hand.

The chance of getting either ace or king in the hole is expressed by the fraction 8/52, the odds against receiving one or other being 5 and 1/2 to 1. In about every 6 and 1/2 deals you should, on an average, get one or other in the hole.

If you do not care to play so conservatively make

your own rules flexible enough to permit a free and easy style of play. For example, the chance of getting ace, king or queen in the hole is expressed by the fraction 12/52, odds against being 3 and 1/3 to 1; you should receive either ace, king or queen in the hole about once in every 4 and 1/3 deals. Ace, king, queen or jack in the hole, 16/52 or odds against of 2 and 1/4 to 1. Ace, king, queen or jack should come your way about once in every 3 and 1/4 deals. The denominator, 52, remains constant; as it is the total number of cards in the deck; the numerator increases by four for every additional card as you descend the scale of values.

The problems that the student of poker can evolve in his mind are many and most interesting. One for example is this: In a game of stud, after dealing one card around "in the hole" and one around, face up, one player has a king showing; what are the odds against this player having a king also "in the hole"?

You, as an opponent know the face value of nine cards (8 on the table face up and your own hole card); there are 43 others; if the king which the player has showing is the only king among the nine cards you know, then, the chance that his "hole" card is a king is 3/43; the chance against it being a king is 40/43; therefore the odds against that player having a king in the "hole" are 40 to 3, about 13 to 1. If however among the nine cards you know there is one other king, then the odds against the player with the king showing having another king in the "hole" are 41 to 2; if there are two other kings known, the odds become 42 to 1. Simple, isn't it?

Here is another one. In a game of stud poker, when an opponent has a pair of nines showing, in the first three cards dealt, including hole card, what are the odds against the hole card also being a nine? Answer: Assume 8 players, an opponent with a pair of nines showing, 6 others and yourself. You know the faces of seventeen cards (16 face up on the table and your own hole card). There remain 35 cards unknown; if your opponent's pair of nines are the only nines you can see, then among the remaining 35 cards are 2 nines and the chance that his hole card is a nine is simply 2/35; the odds against it being a nine are 33 to 2. If, however, there is another nine showing, either face up on the table or your own hole card, then the chance that his hole card is a nine is 1/35 and the odds against are 34 to 1.

And another: In stud poker after receiving two cards, one down and one up, you discover that these cards are ace and king, what are the odds against pairing either in the subsequent dealing of the three remaining cards? Answer: If among the opponents' cards showing, there is no ace or king then among the 43 unknown cards (you know 9 cards, 8 faced on table plus your own hole card among which are your own ace and king) are 6 favorable to pairing, the three aces and the three kings, and 37 unfavorable. The odds against ending the five-card deal with improvement are about 4 to 1.

Under what circumstances should you bet into an exposed pair? This question is a poser, isn't it? However, it need cause no unnecessary worry if a player is well informed regarding the fundamentals of stud poker. As time is of the essence, when this exposed pair appears in an opponent's hand is the all important consideration and is the idea that should govern your offensive.

In an eight-hand game, suppose an opponent has a pair of nines showing after the third card has been dealt and you have a pair better than nines, although not exposed. The odds against this opponent having three nines, as pointed out in a previous paragraph, are 33 to 2 or 16 and 1/2 to 1, under the most favorable conditions, namely, that no other nine is showing in some other player's hand.

If your opponent bets his nines, why shouldn't you

raise him at least once? If this opponent "checks" his nines you still feel that you would be justified in betting into his pair, in view of the fact that the odds against his having threes are 16 and 1/2 to 1, merely calling if you are raised. However, in the cases of certain individual players a "check" under these conditions could be almost prima facie evidence that they really have threes and are merely waiting for an opportunity to raise, so, as noted in a previous page, be careful how you bet against a "check." The principle in poker which encourages the playing of strong hands weakly and weak hands strongly might tell a player to bet his pair of nines, yet "check" three of them. In stud it's "sike" or be "siked"!

After the fourth card has fallen, any exposed pair should be treated with greater respect and this respect should increase as the number of cards dealt increases, assuming of course, that you have not improved your hand.

In a five-card deal the odds against receiving two pairs are 20 to 1 before the deal starts to destroy the pack's symmetry by exposing the cards, however, just as soon as a pair appears, these odds are materially shortened.

If an opponent pairs one of his up cards on the fourth or fifth card dealt and you hold a pair (not showing) higher than this opponent's exposed pair, a conservative appraisal of your relative chances is likely to prove to be the better strategy. Treat this exposed pair with a sort of "reverential awe" as it were, don't be the kind of person who would "rush in where angels fear to tread."

What chance do I have of pairing my hole card?

This question is one that causes stud poker players a lot of worry and makes some addicts lose all perspective in their efforts to catch an elusive ace when they have an ace in the hole.

We are sitting in an eight-hand game of stud, we

will say. One of my opponents has given all evidence of having a pair of kings, backed. I have an ace in the hole. I know that if I pair my hole card, I will beat him, assuming of course, that this opponent does not improve his hand. I am banking on the supposition that he will not have better than a pair of kings in the final showdown, so I proceed to play my ace.

As is customary in nearly all cases where we personally are concerned, we want to give ourselves all the "breaks." This is most natural, so we will postulate a deal in which no ace has shown on the table as any player's first exposed card.

I want to know just what chance I have of pairing my ace in the dealing of the three remaining cards, my first exposed card (2nd card dealt) being, say a five.

After the first round of exposed cards is dealt there is revealed a total of nine cards, my own hole card plus one exposed card for each player in the game. In the unknown cards in the game numbering forty-three are three aces, so the fraction that expresses the probability of being dealt an ace as my third card is 3/43, odds of 40 to 3 or about 13 to 1 against pairing. Let us continue to have hope of pairing this ace in the hole on the fourth round, no ace having shown, and see what the probabilities are.

After the third card is dealt I know the value of seventeen cards, two showing in each player's hand plus my own hole card. There are thirty-five cards unknown, the fraction that expresses the probability of receiving an ace as my fourth card is 3/35, odds against, 32 to 3 or about 11 to 1.

"Hope springs eternal in the human breast" and with quite a large pot by this time as an added incentive, I can think of no reason to justify my quitting at this stage of the game. And still no ace has shown in any player's hand!

After the fourth card has fallen there is a total of twenty-five known cards. Those three aces are among the twenty-seven unknown ones so the fraction of probability is now 3/27; 24 to 3 or 8 to 1 against my pairing my ace in the hole on the fifth card dealt. (Odds, overall, against pairing the ace in 3 draws, about 4 to 1.)

These odds are all based on the fact that no ace has been dealt to any player in the game except the one that I have in the hole. I have given myself all the benefit of the doubt and still the odds are greatly against me. If an ace shows in any opponent's hand it naturally increases the odds against pairing and "makes the going all the tougher."

Supposing all the players in the game except one opponent drop out of the betting after receiving their first exposed cards, let's figure the odds against pairing an ace in the hole. Assuming further that no ace has shown on the first round of exposed cards, the odds are still 13 to 1 against pairing my ace in the hole, on the third card dealt.

With six of my opponents eliminated, the player with the kings still pursues me; at least I am giving him credit for having them.

After receiving my second exposed card and remembering the other cards in the hands of the players who have dropped out of the game, I can place eleven cards, two cards showing in the hand of the opponent still in the game, one in each hand of the six no longer betting and three of my own. In the unknown cards, numbering forty-one, are three aces: the chance that I will receive an ace as my third exposed card is therefore 3/41; odds against, 38 to 3 or about 13 to 1.

I do not get an ace as my third exposed card so I continue in the game. After the dealing of this card I still am able to determine the odds and they are as follows—thirteen known cards, thirty-nine unknown, the fraction expressing the probability of pairing my ace in the hole on the fifth card is therefore 3/39; 36 to 3 or 12 to 1 against making the hand.

Suppose four players stay throughout the betting. What then? The odds are still 13 to 1 against my pairing the ace in the hole on the third card. Remember, eight players are playing!

With only four players staying to draw the fourth card, we find the odds to be as follows: there are thirteen known and thirty-nine unknown cards; the fraction that expresses the probability that I will receive an ace as my fourth card (the third up card) is 3/39; odds against, 36 to 3 or 12 to 1.

After the dealing of the fourth card we find a total of seventeen known and thirty-five unknown cards. The fraction that expresses the probability that I will receive an ace as the fifth card dealt is therefore 3/35, 32 to 3, about 11 to 1 against being so favored. Again, remember that these odds, high as they are, represent my chance under the most favorable conditions, namely, that no ace is "dead" in some other player's hand. If I can place an ace in any other hand, then the odds become almost prohibitive, you might say.

However, "there is another side to the picture." Just because a player gives evidence of having kings, backed, this does not mean that he actually has them. He may be bluffing. The extent of the credence that you place in the evidence that this player offers should be based on several things. One, for instance, is the fact that the odds against receiving a pair back to back are approximately 16 to 1; this is a big handicap in itself. Another is whether this player bets first, merely calls, or raises the pot. Another is the player's propensity for betting or raising. Some players continually play an offensive game, always thinking that their opponents will drop out just because they bet the limit. Learn to play the player as well as the cards. Play the game inductively as well as deductively.

Nearly all of the tactics of card playing set forth so far in this book bear on the consideration of the game from the viewpoint of the value of the first two cards, the comparative value of the hole card being of paramount importance, always. Suppose we indulge in some speculative thinking and consider a few cases from the opposite point of view, namely, after all five cards are dealt.

Even though an astute poker player might consider it a reflection on his intelligence to imply that he might fall heir to a straight or flush sometime, in his effort to beat the game, the idea has such possibilities that it should receive some recognition.

The ability to "take it" has long been admired by those of us possessing less fortitude and the player who can sit through the agony of the dealing of five cards, bearing the brunt of bets, calls and raises, not having a hand until the last card is dealt, deserves a place in history beside that of "the aspiring youth that fired the Ephesian dome." However, a hand of this caliber never "goes begging" for callers as nearly everyone likes to be shown a straight or flush, it bears such eloquent testimony to the holder's belief in a law of compensation. Or could it merely indicate an abiding faith in luck, wishing wells and leprechauns?

Seriously speaking, however, there are times when a smart player will end a five card deal holding a straight or flush, it has been done before and no doubt will be done again. When it does happen, what is more disconcerting than to see opposite you, two pairs on the table?

Strong men have wept, with less provocation, but "crying" over the situation will not change the spots on your opponent's hole card. Has he a full house? Your hoping that he hasn't will not render his hand less potent and the avidity with which he bets does not necessarily mean that he has. If nothing can be done about these players who fill straights and flushes, can't something be done for them?

We will take two cases, similar in detail, possibly, but with the aspect slightly altered. Consider the player who ends a five card deal holding a straight or flush and sees directly opposite, two pairs on the table; then reverse the line of thought and consider the feeling of the player who ends a five card deal with two pairs and finds a 4 straight or 4 flush in an opponent's hand. Either player at different times, no doubt, would have mingled feelings of fear and trepidation regarding the actual strength of the opposing hand and there is no doubt but that the subject is most interesting.

Suppose we consider a stud game, eight players, all staying until the final cards are dealt. You are dealt a flush and one of your opponents has two pairs showing, eights and nines. What are the odds against his having a full house? In an eight hand game after all the cards are dealt, 33 cards are revealed, 32 showing on the table, plus your own hole card. Nineteen cards remain unknown and if the eights and nines in your opponent's hand are the only ones you can place among the known cards, this means that among the 19 unknown ones is the one card necessary to make his full house, either an eight or nine, there being two of each, a total of four available.

Therefore, the fraction that represents the probability that the holder of the two pairs actually has a full house is 4/19; that he has not, 15/19; odds against being 15 to 4 or almost 4 to 1. If, however, you can place one or more eights or nines in the known cards, then the numerator of the fraction of probability would be decreased accordingly, the denominator remaining unchanged; making the odds against the full house greater. As stated elsewhere in this volume, the denominator of the fraction of probability decreases 1 every time a card is faced. The numerator decreases 1, only when the desired card is exposed. With this principle before you, you can figure out for yourself the odds against any given hand at any time.

There is no justice in playing favorites in this treatise on the game so we will now weigh the case of the holder of the two pairs when he views a 4 straight in an opponent's hand. What now? An "inside" straight, or one broken in the middle is twice as hard to fill as one open at either end, so let's make it the "hard way." Suppose this opponent has 4-5-7-8 showing, what are the odds against his having a 6 in the hole?

In this same eight hand game, the total known cards at the end of the five card deal would be 33, assuming that all players stayed throughout. Assuming further that no sixes are in the known cards, means that all four of them are in the cards, unknown. The fraction that expresses the probability that this opponent actually has a straight is, therefore, 4/19; that he has not, 15/19; odds against, being 15 to 4. If among the cards known, you can place one 6, the odds are 16 to 3; if two sixes can be seen, the odds are 17 to 2 or 8 and 1/2 to 1; if three sixes can be placed, the odds are 18 to 1; all against this opponent actually having the straight.

Now, take the case of an opponent having a 4 straight open at either end, say, 8-9-10-J showing. What are the odds against his having either a 7 or queen in the hole? The same eight hand game can still be used as an illustration. 33 known cards, 19 cards unknown; if no sevens or queens can be placed among the cards known, then among the unknown cards are the 8 cards (4 sevens and 4 queens) from which the straight can be completed. Therefore, the chance that the hand is made is 8/19; not made, 11/19; odds against, 11 to 8. If any of the desired cards are showing, decrease the numerator of the fraction accordingly.

The reader can easily figure the odds for himself, against any possible hand, after once learning the trend of the calculations.

Why not continue in our effort to learn more about this interesting game and postulate a deal in which a player is dealt a full house, 3 kings and a pair of fours. He finds three tens in an opponent's hand. What are the odds against this opponent having the case ten in the hole? Obviously, if you cannot place this missing ten in the 33 known cards, 1/19 is the fraction that expresses the probability that this opponent has it in the hole. Odds against, being 18 to 1.

At the end of a five card deal, eight players, one of your opponents has a 4 flush showing, all spades. What is the chance or the odds against his having a spade also, in the hole? 33 known cards, 19 unknown; if, among the cards known there are no spades, this means that among the unknown cards are the 9 spades remaining. 9/19 is the fraction that expresses the probability that the flush is made; 10/19, that it is not made; odds against, 10 to 9. For each spade that can be placed, among the known cards, the numerator of the fraction of probability decreases 1, increasing the odds against the flush actually being held.

At the end of a five card deal, eight players, I find that I have been dealt 4 treys, (it can happen). One of my opponents has a 4 straight flush showing, 5-6-7-8- of diamonds. What are the odds against his having either the 4 or 9 of diamonds in the hole? 33 known cards, 19 unknown. If neither card can be seen among the cards known, then 2/19 is the fraction that represents the probability that the straight flush is made; odds against, 17 to 2. If one of the cards needed for the straight flush can be placed in the known cards, then the odds against the hand being genuine are 18 to 1.

It is interesting to compare the chance of making a flush in draw poker, by drawing one card, with the chance of filling a flush in stud on the last card dealt. As pointed out in an earlier page in this book, the odds against making a flush in draw poker in the draw, by drawing one card, are 4 and 2/9 to 1 and this figure remains constant, irrespective of the number of players, as the deal and draw are "blind." Not so in stud, as exposing the cards changes the percentages entirely.

Hands in the higher brackets, however, that is, two

pairs and upward, are so scarce that they are not likely to cause you any serious inconvenience. Their total number is only 198,180 out of a possible 2,598,960; the odds being 12 to 1 against being dealt a hand higher in value than one pair. You will find that they will almost invariably win, every time you hold one. When your hand has been made and your opponent has his to make, the advantage is certainly yours.

It is exceedingly difficult for two hands in the higher brackets to appear simultaneously or consecutively, assuming of course, that you "called the turn," as this would take the deals out of the category of random events. This is evident from the fact that the fraction of probability illustrative of the chance of one hand of this value appearing being 1/13; 1/13 would likewise be the fraction for the second hand, so the fraction of probability illustrative of the chance of two hands of this strength appearing at the same time would be the product of 1/13x1/13 or 1/169; odds against, being 168 to 1. And the chance of three hands in the higher brackets appearing on the same deal would be the product of 1/13x1/13x1/13 or 1/2197; odds against being, 2,196 to 1.

The odds of 168 to 1 against two hands in the higher brackets appearing in the same deal exist only before the cards are dealt and are changed completely by the dealing of the cards. Likewise, the odds of 12 to 1 against any individual player having a hand of this value are also modified. In some cases, after all the cards are dealt, it would be an impossibility for a player to have a hand of this strength, while at other times it would be a certainty that he has.

Never forget that there is no such thing as an unbeatable hand in poker, the introduction of straights and flushes made this so. Before they were played, 4 aces was the best hand in the deck and "topped" them all, but now, even a Royal Flush can be tied.

Earlier in this book I wrote that the odds against

being dealt a pair, back to back, are 16 to 1. These odds are correct, provided you do not name the particular pair that you are to receive. Of course we all realize that as a matter of practicality no one tries to designate in advance what pair he is to be dealt, backed, in a stud game as there would be no point to the idea. If one were smart enough to be able to do this, I am afraid that there would be too many lifted eye brows, looks askance and possibly, raised chairs, all in a manner too offensive to make the game enjoyable.

The theory of probability, applied to cards, forms one of the most interesting subjects in the field of mathematics, so let's figure the odds against a player naming, in advance, the pair that he will be dealt, back to back. In order to compare these odds with the "16 to 1" occasion, we will assume that the player in question is also sitting on the dealer's immediate left. Being the first one to receive cards permits the deck to remain uniform as all the cards dealt on the first round are faced down.

Suppose this player designates aces as the pair that he is to receive. The chance of being dealt the first ace is $4/52$; the second one, $3/51$; and for the pair, the chance is the product of the two fractions, or $12/2652$; odds against the hand being 220 to 1. In simpler fractions, $1/13 \times 1/17$ or $1/221$, giving you the same answer.

If one were to ask you if there is any difference between cutting two kings, consecutively, from one deck of cards and two kings, consecutively, from two decks, you might be inclined to say the chances are the same in both cases. But, they are not the same, as we shall see. In the first example, the chance of cutting a king from a full deck is $4/52$, for the second king, $3/51$; for the two kings, $4/52 \times 3/51$ or $12/2652$; odds against, 220 to 1. In the second case it is merely the product of $4/52 \times 4/52$ or $16/2704$; odds against, 2,688 to 16 or 168 to 1.

In the first case, the percentage of reduction in

the numerator and the denominator of the fraction of probability is not the same, as the two events are not independent of each other in the sense that they are in the second example.

I'll say the mathematics of cards is interesting!

Although I have used eight players in all examples herein, with the exceptions as noted, the keen observer can use any number of players and obtain results equally satisfactory. A smaller number of players would decrease the number of known cards, changing the odds accordingly, while a larger number of players would increase the number of known cards, also affecting the odds. The fact that the known cards destroy the uniformity of the deck by making the fractions of probability variables instead of constants gives stud poker a "mental twist" that is not even remotely approached by any other card game.

I have saved for the last, question No. 16, in which is asked, "What are the odds against drawing a 'face' card from a full pack in 1 draw? 2 draws? 3 draws?"

This question, while not directly concerned with stud poker, does serve as a splendid example of the universality of the application of the Theory of Probability when certain factors are known in advance.

In the case of a problem in probability when only one chance is given you, such as part one of question No. 16, it is sufficient merely to find the fraction of probability illustrative of the chance of success and deduct it from 1. The resultant fraction indicates the probability of failure.

In solving a problem in probability where a plurality of chances is involved, the proper way to arrive at the correct answer is to find the product of the fractions of probability illustrative of failure and deduct this product from 1. The resultant fraction indicates the probability of success.

In the consideration of the first part of question No. 16, we know that there are 12 "face" cards in a total of

74

52. Therefore, the fraction that illustrates the probability of drawing a "face" card in one draw is 12/52 or 3/13; of not drawing the card, 10/13. Odds against, being 10 to 3. The first part of question No. 16 is simple because there are only two possibilities involved.

Part two of question No. 16 is more complicated because you are given two chances and there is a possibility that you might miss on both of them.

The answer to part two is 1—(10/13) 2. One minus the second power of 10/13 equals 1—(10/13x10/13) or 1—100/169. Odds against, being 100 to 69 or about 10 to 7.

To answer part three of question No. 16, we find the third power of 10/13 and deduct it from 1. 1—(10/13x 10/13x10/13) equals 1—1000/2197; or 1197 to 1000; practically, 6 to 5 in favor of drawing the desired card.

Therefore, the direct and categorical answer to question No. 16 follows:

In one draw, odds against, 3 and 1/3 to 1
In two draw, odds against,   10 to 7
In three draw, odds in favor,   **6 to 5**

Suppose we consider this question at greater length as it is very interesting and gives us chance to appraise the different answers that might, conceivably, be given. It might be said, by some, that if the fraction of probability illustrative of success, in one draw, is 3/13; then chance of success in three draws would be 3x3/13 or 9/13; 4/13 being the chance of failure, odds in favor, 9 to 4 or 2 and 1/4 to 1. But this line of reasoning is incorrect as it fails to take into consideration the concurrent chance of failure and will, eventually, give you a fraction of probability, illustrative of success, greater than one, which is an absurdity.

Let me explain further, suppose you were given 6 chances to "cut" a face card from a pack, would your chance of success be 6x3/13 or 18/13? Surely not! Because 18/13 is greater than unity, and unity is equivalent to certainty, whereas, even in 1,000 draws there is a possibility of failure. Therefore, we must find an equation which will give us a fraction less than one; a fraction whose numerator is less than its denominator.

In 6 draws your chance of "cutting" a face card from a full pack is 1 minus the sixth power of 10/13; odds in favor, about 4 to 1.

"When mother hands sonny her last two bucks and sends him down to the corner store to win the rent in the stud game, sonny should have some guidance as to whether his jacks up are betting into the midst of three tens across the table or merely facing tens over treys. Or could he be challenging kings over tens?" writes Mr. Westbrook Pegler.

To expect sonny to be able to run two dollars into rent money, which would probably be at least fifteen or twenty times the amount of the original investment requires nerve, verve and temerity; however, it has been done. To expect sonny to win merely enough to pay the telephone or gas bills would be within the bounds of reason, especially if sonny "should have the advantage of expert coaching." Let's look the hands over and see what the problem is that seems to be standing between sonny and an irate landlord.

In order that we may be able, arithmetically, to give sonny assistance that might possibly be of value to him, we must first ascertain the number of players in the game, so we will deduce as follows—It seems as though the young man has gotten into a stud game composed of eight players, including himself, and after several deals in which he found the boys ready and willing to back their hands to the limit, a situation relished by a careful player, finds himself possessed of jacks up. In fact he had jacks backed, bet them properly and in addition garnered a pair of fives. After the fifth card had been dealt to sonny his hand consisted of jacks and fives with the off card being a seven.

Pete's hand, directly across the table, in the order in which the cards were dealt, consisted of a pair of tens, trey and king exposed, the hole card being the one that interested sonny, no end. Sonny's problem, as stated by Mr. Pegler, was to decide whether Pete had three tens, kings up or tens up.

It so happened that all the players on this particular round stayed to the finish, a most unusual event in an eight-hand game, but there they were, just the same. Sonny felt greatly relieved as the last cards were dealt as after the final appraisal of all the hands no one but Pete could offer any serious opposition to his jacks up. After looking the table over, sonny saw that there were no treys, kings or tens showing on the board except those in Pete's "up" cards so he did some quick calculating.

He knew the value of 33 cards, four faced up in each player's hand, plus his own hole card. In the remaining cards, unknown, numbering 19, were two tens; the chance, therefore, of Pete having a ten in the hole is expressed by the fraction 2/19; the chance against Pete having a ten in the hole 17/19. Odds against Pete's having three tens, 17 to 2 or 8 and 1/2 to 1. If among the known cards, sonny could see one ten in a player's hand, other than Pete's, then the fraction of probability would change. Pete's chance of then having the case ten in the hole would be 1/19 or odds of 18 to 1 against his having threes.

Sonny continues his calculations after somewhat eliminating the probability of Pete's having three tens and fixes his attention on the probability of kings up, which would be bad for sonny unless he could bluff Pete out of the pot. As sonny could locate no king except the one among Pete's exposed cards, this meant that among the 19 unknown cards were 3 kings. The fraction that expresses the probability that Pete has a king in the hole is 3/19; that Pete has no king in the hole, 16/19; odds against the king in the hole being 16 to 3 or 5 and 1/3 to 1. These odds would also prevail in the case of figuring the chance of a trey being in the hole as there was an equal number of both kings and treys available.

If, however, among the known cards there was one king in addition to the one showing in Pete's cards, the fraction of probability changed to 2/19 in favor of Pete's hole card being a king; odds of 17 to 2 or 8 and 1/2 to 1 against.

If there were two known kings in addition to the one in Pete's hand, the chance that Pete's hole card was a king was expressed by the fraction 1/19 or odds of 18 to 1 against his having a king in the hole. Sonny knew that he could substitute "treys" for "kings" and his calculations would be just as valid as under the same conditions, the same odds would present themselves.

Suppose we look the situation over again and try to figure for sonny his chance of ultimately winning this pot. Pete needs to have either 3 tens or kings up, to win. Assume that there were no tens or kings showing except in Pete's hand.

This meant that at the best, Pete had only 5 chances out of 19 to win, there being two tens and three kings in a total of 19 unknown cards. The fraction 5/19 expresses the probability of Pete's having either ten or king in the hole, 14/19, that he does not; odds against 14 to 5 or about 3 to 1. Note how the numerator of the fraction of probability increases as the number of chances, favorable, increases. No doubt you recall that in an earlier page I said that the denominator of the fraction of probability decreases one for every card faced while the numerator decreases one, only when the desired card is exposed. Supposing the number of players in the game had been seven, instead of eight; the number of unknown cards or the denominator of our fraction would have been 23; if six players, 27 and so on. If the number of players had been nine, the unknown cards then would have been 15; which would have been the denominator. If the number of players

78

had been ten, the number of unknown cards would have been 11; this number then being the denominator.

All of these elaborate calculations of course, cannot tell sonny the value of the card that Pete has in the hole but they might serve the purpose of causing sonny to think about the probabilities involved and to govern his betting accordingly. Knowing the chances of making certain hands will give a player at least the poise necessary in the face of danger and at the same time will permit him to exercise more courage in the presence of merely apparent disaster.

Sonny, no doubt, would not insist that he be endowed with infallibility in the matter of trying to determine what card an opponent has in the hole. The best that can be done for any stud player is to give him certain information about card playing, which, of course, cannot always be taken or applied literally.

The writer has often sat in games where situations as described by Mr. Pegler have been encountered and has heard some player remark, upon the occasion that an opponent had the winning card in the hole, that the odds against this opponent being so favored were "1000 to 1" or some other figure equally ridiculous, the truth being that the actual odds were maybe 4 or 5 to 1, against the opponent having the winning card, certainly not an insurmountable handicap.

Mr. Pegler does not tell us how sonny came out on this interesting deal but, offhand, I would say that his jacks up were good.

On the Subject of "Netods"

and

THE SMALL PAIR, BACKED

vs.

A K COMBINATION OR "ACE IN THE HOLE"

In the compilation of statistics, upon which is to be based the correct mode of play in stud poker, it is necessary for the devotee of the game to understand certain mathematical data even though it be arbitrary. When a theory in probability is expressed mathematically, it must, of course, be definite and we must be careful in our choice of words so that we will convey the proper meaning.

It does not necessarily follow that the thing which most probably will happen, will always happen in individual cases. For instance, a player can lose in stud poker even though the odds are in his favor. Likewise, he can win with the odds against his doing so. He might win a pot without improving his hand in subsequent deals and he might lose, even though his hand is bettered, in normal course of play.

With these facts firmly fixed in our minds, suppose we consider the ultimate odds that a player with a pair, backed, receives in an eight hand session of stud.

I am now pleased to present, for which I believe to be the first time in any book on the subject of stud poker, what I shall denominate "netods." (Combination of net and odds.)

The netods are "three-dimensional," in that they reconcile, 1st. the probability of improvement by a player holding a backed pair; 2nd. the probability of some one of his opponents ending the 5 card deal with a hand better than this backed pair; 3rd. the odds that the holder of this backed pair receives in the betting. Numbers 1 and 2 constitute what is known in card parlance as card odds. No. 3 is known as money odds. Numbers 2 and 3 are variables, being contingent on the number of opponents. We will consider No. 1 a constant.

Unless these 3 component parts are combined in a manner in which all parts share in determining the true status of a player, correct play is almost impossible. As an example, suppose the card odds are 3 to 1 against a player receiving the best hand in a 4 hand game, the money odds, or the odds that the pot bets him, as it were, are 3 to 1 in his favor. Therefore, the bet is an even one. The money odds received compensate for the card odds against him.

Balancing the money odds against the card odds gives the netods and unless the netods are ascertained, knowledge of whether or not the bet is sound remains unknown.

In the first issue of this book (as also in the previous chapter in this one) I show the probabilities of deuces, fives, eights, jacks and aces being outdrawn by from 1 to 7 opponents, inclusive. However, space limitation prevented taking into account the concurrent probability of improvement by the holders of these backed pairs. When these two factors are measured against, or in conjunction with, each other then the true card odds are known. When the true card odds are measured against the money odds, then the netods tell the final story.

We will assume that the holder of a backed pair will lose if either of two things happens, namely, failure to improve his pair, or the making of a hand, by some opponent, of value higher than this backed pair. (If no player improves, the holder of the backed pair wins, ipso facto. If all improve, the odds still favor the backed pair.)

In all of the following equations, the fractions within the brackets indicate the separate probabilities as defined in the previous paragraph. These fractions indicate the probability of the backed pair in question losing. One minus their product indicates the probability of winning. The probability of winning times total stakes equals netods.

I have formulated the following equation to express the manner in which these 3 factors should be considered, mathematically, in determining the probability of a backed pair winning in stud poker.

1—(product of separate probabilities of losing) times total stakes equals netods.

The probability of improving a backed pair is a moot question because, in stud, a priori calculations are always modified by the exposed cards. With this knowledge before us we will have to assume that a certain fraction is correct and use it accordingly. I give you the fraction 1/4 as being fair under the circumstances; which means that the fraction 3/4 indicates the chance of no improvement. Odds, overall, against improvement, 3 to 1.

Therefore, in the case of the holder of deuces, backed, with probability of no improvement represented by the fraction 3/4; against one opponent, with the probability of this opponent making a hand of value higher than the deuces represented by the fraction 1/2; with 2 representing the total stakes; the netods are expressed by the equation $[1—(3/4 \times 1/2)] \times 2$ equals 1 and 1/4 to 1, in favor of the deuces.

In the case of the holder of fives, backed; against one opponent; $[1—(3/4 \times 1/3)] \times 2$ equals 1 and 1/2 to 1, in favor of the fives.

In the case of the holder of eights, backed; against one opponent; $[1—(3/4 \times 1/4)] \times 2$ equals 1 and 5/8 to 1, in favor of the eights.

In the case of the holder of jacks, backed; against one opponent; $[1—(3/4 \times 1/6)] \times 2$ equals 1 and 3/4 to 1, in favor of the jacks.

In the case of the holder of aces, backed; against one opponent; 1—(3/4x1/13)x2 equals 2 to 1. in favor of the aces.

Suppose we phrase the idea in another manner and present the theory in a different light. We will take the case of the holder of fives, backed, against 6 opponents. What is the probability of winning or the card odds for or against the holder of fives, backed, against 6 opponents? Also, the netods?

The probability of winning, thru improvement is 1/4; thru failure of any opponent to make a hand of higher value than fives, 1/12. The chance that the fives will not win on the one hand is 3/4, and on the other, 11/12. The chance that the fives will lose in both cases is 11/16. Therefore, the chance that the fives will win, one way or the other, is 1—11/16 or 5/16; odds against, being 2 and 1/5 to 1. The netods are probability of winning x total stakes or 5/16x7, equals netods in favor of the fives of 2 and 1/5 to 1.

How about the case of the holder of jacks, backed, against 3 opponents? The probability of winning, thru improvement, is likewise 1/4, thru failure of any opponent making a hand of higher value than the jacks, 4/7. The probability of losing, either thru lack of improvement or the making of a hand by some opponent, of value higher than jacks, 3/4 and 3/7, respectively. Therefore, the chance of winning, one way or the other, is 1—(3/4x3/7) or odds in favor of 2 and 1/8 to 1. The netods equals 19/28x4 or netods in favor of 2 and 5/7 to 1.

The foregoing figures are verified by the following recapitulation:

RECAPITULATION.

Deuces Backed

Opponents		Card Odds Win	Card Odds Lose	Money Odds For	Netods For
1	1—(3/4x1/2) x2 equals	1 and 2/3-1		Even	1 and 1/4-1
2	1—(3/4x3/4) x3 equals		1 and 2/7-1	2-1	1 and 1/3-1
3	1—(3/4x7/8) x4 equals		2-1	3-1	1 and 1/3-1
4	1—(3/4x15/16) x5 equals		2 and 2/5-1	4-1	1 and 1/2-1
5	1—(3/4x31/32) x6 equals		2 and 2/3-1	5-1	1 and 5/8-1
6	1—(3/4x63/64) x7 equals		2 and 7/8-1	6-1	1 and 3/4-1
7	1—(3/4x127/128) x8 equals		3-1	7-1	2-1

Fives Backed

Opponents	Card Odds Win	Card Odds Lose	Money Odds For	Netods For
1 — (3/4x1/3)x2 equals	3-1		Even	1 and 1/2-1
2 — (3/4x5/9)x3 equals	1 and 2/5-1		2-1	1 and 3/4-1
3 — (3/4x19/27)x4 equals		1 and 1/8-1	3-1	2-1
4 — (3/4x65/81)x5 equals		1 and 1/2-1	4-1	2-1
5 — (3/4x7/8)x6 equals		2-1	5-1	2-1
6 — (3/4x11/12)x7 equals		2 and 1/5-1	6-1	2 and 1/5-1
7 — (3/4x20/21)x8 equals		2 and 1/2-1	7-1	2 and 2/7-1

Eights Backed

Opponents	Card Odds Win	Card Odds Lose	Money Odds For	Netods For
1 — (3/4x1/4)x2 equals	4 and 1/3-1		Even	1 and 5/8-1
2 — (3/4x7/16)x3 equals	2-1		2-1	2-1
3 — (3/4x37/64)x4 equals	1 and 1/3-1		3-1	2 and 1/4-1
4 — (3/4x17/25)x5 equals	Even		4-1	2 and 1/2-1
5 — (3/4x13/17)x6 equals		1 and 1/3-1	5-1	2 and 1/2-1
6 — (3/4x33/40)x7 equals		1 and 2/3-1	6-1	2 and 3/5-1
7 — (3/4x7/8)x8 equals		2-1	7-1	2 and 2/3-1

Jacks Backed

Opponents	Win	Card Odds Lose	Money Odds For	Netods For
1—(3/4x1/6)x2 equals	7-1		Even	1 and 3/4-1
2 1—(3/4x11/36)x3 equals	3 and 1/3-1		2-1	2 and 1/3-1
3 1—(3/4x3/7)x4 equals	2 and 1/8-1		3-1	2 and 5/7-1
4 1—(3/4x1/2)x5 equals	1 and 2/3-1		4-1	3 and 1/8-1
5 1—(3/4x46/77)x6 equals	1 and 1/4-1		5-1	3 and 1/3-1
6 1—(3/4x31/46)x7 equals	Even		6-1	3 and 1/2-1
7 1—(3/4x5/7)x8 equals		1 and 1/6-1	7-1	3 and 5/7-1

Aces Backed

Opponents	Win	Card Odds Lose	Money Odds For	Netods For
1—(3/4x1/13)x2 equals	16 and 1/3-1		Even	2-1
2 1—(3/4x25/169)x3 equals	8-1		2-1	2 and 2/3-1
3 1—(3/4x46/219)x4 equals	5 and 1/3-1		3-1	3 and 1/3-1
4 1—(3/4x78/285)x5 equals	3 and 4/5-1		4-1	4-1
5 1—(3/4x1/3)x6 equals	3-1		5-1	4 and 1/2-1
6 1—(3/4x3/8)x7 equals	2 and 5/9-1		6-1	5-1
7 1—(3/4x13/31)x8 equals	2 and 1/5-1		7-1	5 and 1/2-1

86

In games of chance and skill, odds "move in a mysterious way, their wonders to perform." In poker, for instance, we must distinguish between the card odds and the netods. If we say that the card odds are 5 to 1 in favor of a certain hand winning, it means that the chance of winning is 5/6, or 5 in 6. This does not mean certitude. But if we say that the netods are in favor of certain hands winning, under given conditions, it is equivalent to saying that the players holding these hands may look forward to a profit, over a period of time.

I repeat, if the netods are represented by a proper fraction, a fraction less than one, it means that the bettor is contributing to the pool more money than the risk deserves. If the netods are represented by an improper fraction, one more than unity, the amount risked is not too much for the chance involved.

On a number of occasions you will find that even though the card odds are against certain pairs winning, the netods are in their favor, which makes the bet sound. In these cases you will observe that the money odds compensate for the disparity of card odds.

Never forget, however, that all through the labyrinth of odds, there runs the human element and psychology of the game, which, at times, seem to dwarf its mathematical calculations. Study these factors, also. Look for certain tell-tale incidents which, to the student of the game, will serve as beacons, guiding him on the road toward gain and implementing his knowledge of proper mode of play.

(In discussing the relative merits of deuces, backed, vs. the ace-king combination or "ace in the hole," these values will be considered from both theoretical and practical viewpoints.)

The theoretical side of the case of the Ace-King Combination vs. Deuces backed.

Apropos—Comes now counsel for the Deuces, known hereafter as the Defendant, who insists that the Ace-

King Combination, known hereafter as the Plaintiff, establish its superiority over the Defendant by virtue of having paired either Ace or King in the dealing of the three remaining cards. The Defendant claims that the Plaintiff may not strengthen his argument by introducing testimony showing that the Plaintiff defeated the Defendant by having made a pair merely higher than deuces, as this could have been done irrespective of the value of the Plaintiff's first two cards.

In other words, the greater objective value of the Ace-King Combination, per se, must be established by the Plaintiff. The Court agrees with Counsel for the Defendant and instructs the jury (which in this case shall be the reader) accordingly.

In reviewing the evidence presented by the Plaintiff, counsel for the Defense calls the attention of the jury to the thought that great stress is placed on the fact that once in about every three deals that a player starts with an Ace-King Combination, either the Ace or King will be paired in the dealing of the three remaining cards. With this idea in mind it is easy to see that if A and B play "head and head," with the stipulation that A be given a pair of deuces, backed, and B an Ace-King Combination as initial hands, the netods are 1 and 1/2 to 1 in favor of A. $(1-(3/4x1/3)x2.)$

The point cannot be made that B can win by pairing cards other than the Ace or King, as this would be outside the scope of the argument. (The "sliding scale" value of hands in the same class can also be seen when it is realized that queens could be substituted for deuces without strengthening A's chances, because if the Ace or King in B's hand were paired, queens would be just as impotent as deuces, whereas if the Ace or King were not paired, deuces would be just as potent as queens.)

It might also be remarked that A, with an initial holding of deuces, backed, will improve his pair about 1 time in 4. Therefore, in any given series of say, 100 deals, under the foregoing rules, A, with his small pair, backed, should defeat B with the Ace-King Combination on an average of approximately 75 times.

The practical side of the case of the Ace-King Combination vs. Deuces Backed.

The practical side of the question boils down to this: Permitting B to win, irrespective of the pair that he makes in the 5 card deal, so long as his hand is better than his opponent's, still finds B at a disadvantage. The first equation in the Recapitulation, under Deuces, backed, gives us the answer. That the backed deuces will win, through improvement, 1/4; that they will win because one opponent failed to receive a hand better than a pair of deuces, 1/2. That the backed deuces will win, one way or the other, $1-(3/4 \times 1/2) \times 2$ equals card odds in their favor of 1 and 2/3 to 1. Netods in favor of the deuces, 1 and 1/4 to 1.

This means that the fraction of probability illustrative of the backed deuces winning is 5/8. Therefore, in any given series of 100 deals, A, with the backed deuces, should defeat B with the Ace-King Combination on an average of approximately 62 times.

Counsel for the Defense now calls the attention of the Court to a statement made earlier in the trial to the effect that these cases would be argued both as to fact as well as to theory and asks for more time in which to present the practical side of the question in regard to the case of the "Ace in the Hole" vs. Deuces, backed. The Court, being a practical man as well as a devotee of stud poker, cannot see where anyone is being deprived of his rights so agrees to the Defense continuing.

(Five players will illustrate the point involved.)

Counsel for the Defense then introduces witnesses denominated A, B, C, D and E, who agree to play a game of stud in order that certain points may be illustrated. The cards are shuffled, cut properly, then dealt around. A, being dealer, gets a deuce up. B, C, D and E receive K, 8, 10, and Q, respectively. B, high with the King, bets first and is called by C, D and E. Up to this time A has not looked at his hole card as he has been busy watching the play. Should he hope that his hidden card is another deuce, or would it be better to have an "Ace in the Hole"?

A's mind is a jumble of thoughts at this juncture as he seems to be in a "tough spot." Which card would be better for him "in the hole"?

In view of the layout A decides that his only salvation is in his hole card. He realizes that if his hole card is an Ace, the odds against pairing this Ace in the dealing of the 3 remaining cards are about 4 to 1, assuming that no other Ace can be "spotted" somewhere. He also reasons that with 4 opponents he will need at least a pair to win. Even though none of his opponents raised the pot, this would not be proof positive of lack of a pair, but even so, A feels morally certain that Ace high is the best out against him.

A also knows that the fraction of probability illustrative of the chance of any one of his opponents having a pair, backed, is $1/15$; no pair, $14/15$. Odds against, 14 to 1.

Therefore, the chance of there being a pair among 4 opponents, all faced cards being unlike, is 1 minus the fourth power of $14/15$ or odds against a pair among B, C, D and E of about 3 to 1.

A continues his reasoning after eliminating the probability of there being a pair out against him. He knows that C, D and E are too well versed in the game to stay against the initial bet by the King without having a card in the hole at least as high or higher than the highest card showing. Which makes it probable that at least one of the three has an "Ace in the hole."

A also reasons that with an Ace in the hand of one of his opponents his chance of getting an Ace to pair his own mythical "Ace in the Hole" is materially lessened. (Remember that A has not yet looked at his hole card.) A continues to think the situation over, he suddenly realizes that if he has an "Ace in the Hole," plus the probable Ace among his opponents, only 2 aces were left and another ace would have to be gotten "the hard way." In the light of this reasoning where would the percentage be in having an "Ace in the Hole?"

A continues to ponder the problem. Then the thought occurs that maybe some other card "in the hole" might be of greater advantage to him. But surely, no card of value lower than a king; except possibly a deuce. Here was a thought! If he had a deuce "in the hole," then he would have a pair, and considering the probability of an Ace "in the hole" somewhere among B, C, D and E, A reasons correctly that his chance of improving his backed pair would be much better than his chance of getting the 2nd ace. And if he improved his deuces he would have a superlative hand!

So, why not wish for a deuce? That's it! Wish for a deuce and if he has one "in the hole," raise the pot! At the moment that A bets for the first time, he gets odds in the pot of 5 to 1 in his favor. His own ante plus the bets of his 4 opponents. If he has a pair of deuces, he realizes that its value decreases as the number of opponents increases. He also realizes that if he merely calls, all of his opponents stay to draw the 3rd card.

A reasons that at least two of his opponents would drop if he raised the pot. His opponents are good players, they know that, as a unit, they could probably defeat the raiser but in stud there is no "collective bargaining," neither is there "place" or "show" money, so in order to achieve parity with any player who indicates strength (in this case, A) it would be necessary for the 4 opponents of this player to win (in this case) on the basis of 4 to 1, in order that these opponents, individually, might share in an equable distribution of winnings. (This last feature, to a great extent, nullifies the desire that players have of calling bets in poker unless their hands possess real value.)

A looks at his hole card, finds it to be a deuce, and raises the limit. Because his opponents are good players they decide to conserve their funds for an occasion when a raise might be in order for them so A wins the pot by raising, even though dealing 5 cards to all in the game might have caused him to lose.

(Counsel for the Defense also refuses to permit the Plaintiff to introduce testimony showing that the holder of the "Ace in the hole" defeated the Defendant by pairing a card other than the "Ace in the hole.")

As further evidence in behalf of the value of deuces backed, suppose we subject the "Ace in the hole" to the same mathematical "scalpel" that we used on the deuces in the preceding recapitulation.

To be the "drama" card of stud, the "Ace in the hole" must be paired in the dealing of the three remaining cards, otherwise it remains just a high card which avails the holder nothing in the face of probably made pairs in a 6, 7 or 8 hand game.

Suppose we consider the netods for or against the holder of an "Ace in the hole" in an 8 hand game, so that we can compare its effectiveness with deuces backed, figured on the same basis.

In this connection, the netods are also "three-dimensional" in that they likewise reconcile (1st) the probability of pairing the "Ace in the hole" in the dealing of the 3 remaining cards; (2nd) the probability of some opponent making a hand higher in value than this "Ace in the hole"; (3rd) the odds that the holder of the "Ace in the hole" receives in the betting.

The same qualifying conditions are also present as set forth in connection with the backed pair.

We will assume that the holder of the "Ace in the hole" will lose if either of two things happens, namely, failure to pair the Ace, or the making of a hand, by some opponent, of greater value than Ace high.

The odds against pairing an "Ace in the hole" in three draws are approximately 4 to 1; which makes the fraction of probability illustrative of success, 1/5; 4/5 indicates the probable failure. The probability that one opponent will make a hand of value, pair or better is 1/2; therefore, the netods in favor of the "Ace in the hole" may be expressed by the following equation; 1—(4/5x1/2)x2 equals card odds in favor of the Ace, 1 and 1/2 to 1; netods in favor, 1 and 1/5 to 1.

(The recapitulation follows on page 94).

"Ace In the Hole."

Opponents	Card Odds		Money Odds For	Netods For
	Win	Lose		
1 1—(4/5x1/2)x2 equals	1 and 1/2-1		Even	1 and 1/5-1
2 1—(4/5x3/4)x3 equals		1 and 1/2-1	2-1	1 and 1/5-1
3 1—(4/5x7/8)x4 equals		2 and 1/3-1	3-1	1 and 1/5-1
4 1—(4/5x15/16)x5 equals		3-1	4-1	1 and 1/4-1
5 1—(4/5x31/32)x6 equals		3 and 4/9-1	5-1	1 and 7/20-1
6 1—(4/5x63/64)x7 equals		3 and 12/17-1	6-1	1 and 1/2-1
7 1—(4/5x127/128)x8 equals		3 and 9/11-1	7-1	1 and 13/20-1

It can easily be seen from a comparison of the netods, that the backed deuces have the advantage. The odds against improving the deuces being 3 to 1, while the odds against pairing the "Ace in the hole" are 4 to 1; both figured on the basis of a three card draw.

In addition, and this is most important, the contemplated hand in the case of deuces backed, is two pairs or better, in the case of the "Ace in the hole," it is merely a single pair.

Ace-King backed—100 situations.

Deuces backed—100 situations.

Which is the better hand?

Which hand should win the more money?

8 hand game.

The above hands are not to be held simultaneously by different players, as set forth previously in this book, but are to be held by the same player at different times.

Player A sits in his usual Wednesday night stud session and holds Ace down, King up, 100 times. He also plays in a Saturday night game and on 100 occasions holds deuces, backed.

The real value attached to Ace-King combination as an initial hand lies in pairing either in the dealing of the 3 remaining cards; odds against, being 2 to 1. The odds against improving a backed pair, 3 to 1.

Therefore, when A holds Ace-King combination he will pair one or the other about 33 times in every 100; when he holds deuces, backed, he will improve them about 25 times in every 100. Now, suppose we examine the concurrent chances of the opponents of A, both when A has the Ace-King combination and when he has deuces backed.

The odds are 1 and 1/3 to 1 against there being a hand of value 2 pairs or better among the seven opponents of A; which makes the chances of success 3/7. This fraction applies to the situation in both cases, as the difference in the known cards would not make any material change in the overall probabilities. This means that on an average of about 43 times in every 100 deals some one of seven players will end the 5 card draw holding two pairs or better.

It is reasonable to presume that on a number of occasions during the course of the 100 deals, improvement on the part of A with his A-K combination or deuces backed, will occur coincidentally with the making of two pairs or better on the part of some opponent. In these cases, deuces backed, should fare better than the A-K combination, because the deuces could be "upped" to a hand in the higher brackets more easily than could the A-K combination.

On the occasions that A did not improve either his A-K combination or deuces backed, the backed deuces would at least get a "draw" with the A-K combination, because at any time that an opponent of A held a hand that could beat the deuces, this hand would also beat the A-K combination.

The foregoing arguments are concerned with the positive features of the game, looked at from the offensive angle. Suppose we view the idea from the negative or defensive side of the question.

Any student of stud must know that it is just as important to play a strong defensive game when poor cards are held, as it is to play a strong offensive game when you hold good hands, reserving the right, of course, to vary these tactics as necessity demands.

Player B sits in both games against A and holds merely average cards. B has read "How to Win at Stud Poker" and realizes that defensive play certainly has no small part in stud, so in which circumstance would B be the more likely to lose to A?

By analogy, we can invoke the same line of reasoning in behalf of the other opponents of A in the same games, assuming, of course, that all the players in the games understand the fundamentals of stud.

B, with average cards, knowing that unless his hole card at least equals in value the highest card showing in an opponent's hand, would be more likely to turn his hand against a king than against a deuce. In neither case, of course, would B know the value of A's hole card, therefore, the deuce up would invite assault while the king would repel it, emphasizing the fact that B would be more likely to play against the deuce than to play against the king.

In refusing to play against the king but in playing against the deuce, B places himself in the position of being more likely to lose to the deuces, backed, than to lose to the Ace-King combination.

B would probably be beaten in sight by A's king, without taking A's hole card into consideration, whereas it would not at all be self-evident that A's deuce up indicated that he had deuces, backed. Therefore, over a period of time, A, with deuces backed, would get a better play than he would with ace-king combination, with consequent greater opportunity for gain.

The examples just quoted do no violence to mathematical probability, nor are they contrary to good poker-playing strategy. They *could* happen very easily and should not outrage anyone's sense of justice in regard to stud. Even though they have been quoted more "to point a moral or adorn a tale" than to be followed literally in all cases, they certainly call attention to the fact that in poker the ultimate strength or weakness of your hand is not disclosed instantaneously.

The worth of a stud hand is unfolded successively, which, with its concomitant of four rounds of "pressure" betting instead of two, as in draw, entitles the game to study and investigation.

In his closing speech to the jury, Counsel for the Defense claims that the Plaintiff has not made a case, and asks for a verdict for his client.

What does the jury say?

The Philosophy and Ethics of
Stud Poker

There is also a philosophical side to stud poker. Oftentimes a player's game is ruined due to the fact that he persists in sitting in those games where the limit is too steep to permit a free and easy style of play. He becomes so worried over the impossibility of breaking what he thinks is a run of "bad luck" that he loses his ability to diagnose the simplest hands and, as a consequence, becomes prey to fear. Then, this player should use good judgment and resolve never to play cards for any sizable stakes in any game where the other participants are greatly his superiors in their ability to lose consistently without feeling the losses financially.

Seek games in which the personal equation of finances is nearly even. This should not be difficult and, furthermore, should be the aim of those to whom poker is merely a pastime rather than a means of existence. Play in games which have the limit so arranged as not to take too large a percentage of your capital at any one time. By all means play limit games. Do not play "no-limit" ones, as this is the feature that ultimately ruins most players, robbing the game of that zestful pleasure without which it becomes merely an expression of gambling.

Failure to establish a limit in a friendly poker game works like a two-edged sword. One player with almost unlimited capital places his assets at the mercy of possibly 6, 7 or 8 opponents whose total capital may not exceed one-twentieth or one-fiftieth that of the wealthier man. Even though the wealthier man, say, with his capital of $200.00 can make me lay down a better hand, backed by my meager capital of $2.00, at the same time he exposes his resources to attack all out of proportion to his chances to recover. The establishment of a limit, either of the individual bet that can be made at any one time or a limit to the loss that may be sustained in any one game, acts as a "governor" and is more consonant with equity and fairness.

As in nearly every other form of human endeavor, all things being equal, the person with the most capital will nearly always win, so, also in stud poker, will you find persons who seem to take delight in punishing the ones in the game who can least afford to lose and then, stud poker, becomes brutal.

In philosophy there is no such thing as "luck" as a matter of objective truth, independent of the mind as a reality. "Luck" is purely subjective, in the eye of the beholder. We say a man is "lucky" just because certain things happen to him which are favorable. We know nothing of the details of reverses which have occurred in his lifetime under possibly identical conditions. We see him maybe for only the one time that the "gods of fortune" have smiled on his efforts, and erroneously conclude that "lucky" is the word that most aptly describes this or that individual. The amount of "bad luck" that a player has over a period of time is practically negligible. He holds average cards and his winning or losing is contingent on how he plays them. He will win if he is the better player, and if on particular occasions when, in his opinion, "luck" seems to be against him, he will not lose nearly as often, or as much money, as will some player who trusts to blind chance and discounts all theory of probability.

A smart player need never worry about where the "popcorn" is coming from, so long as he can find individuals who have never heard of and care less about percentages pertaining to the dealing of stud poker.

Stud poker, being based on the winning of pots, each pot being founded on an indefinite number of cards, and not on the winning of tricks as in the game of bridge, with an arbitrary number of cards on each deal, for instance, does not in the course of play create the "artificial pattern formation" so often encountered in those games of whist origin.

There is no subconscious effort on the part of stud players to create a well nigh indestructible "stacking" of the deck, through the mechanics of play that is found in a number of other card games.

To a certain degree, draw poker is affected by this "artificial pattern formation," but only to a minor extent, whereas in stud there can obviously be no effort made by the players, assuming that they are honest, to stack the cards in any manner except according to the way that chance and probability have thrown them together.

A card game that is based on the winning of tricks, necessitating the "following of suit" as the cards are played, is practically certain to create rock-ribbed "artificial suit formations" which subsequent shuffling does not dissipate.

Viewed through the lorgnette of careful reasoning, we must reach the conclusion, namely, that "luck" or any other exterior factor counts for very little in the successful playing of stud poker, and it is from this angle that I addressed myself to the task of setting forth in some detail the more salient facts regarding this most pleasant game.

In recording my principles for playing winning stud poker, I have been plain in my statements, I endeavored to avoid that abstract form that so many books of instruction on various subjects possess, and I also tried to escape being pontifical, as "argument from authority is the weakest of all arguments."

However, I do not pretend to infallibility in the realm of cards. I also realize that there is an indefinable

100

abstractness about them that almost evades capture, but I do know that dividends in pleasure beyond your fondest hope await those of you who approach the subject knowing something of the difficulties involved and the pitfalls to be avoided.

Never forget the main admonition in this book, namely, unless your hole card, paired, will beat any "up" card in an opponent's hand if that "up" card were paired, throw your hand in the discard. Appraise the hands as soon as the dealer has given each player his first card, faced up. Another way of saying the rule is, unless your hole card is as high or higher than the highest card showing among your opponents, throw your hand away. Unless the odds in the betting and your chances of improvement warrant it, play only "overlay" cards. Over a period of time, the probabilities are that your opponent will pair his king, showing, as often as you will pair your queen in the hole.

Never quarrel with a player just because he enters a pot when you think he has no business in it. The money that he pays is his own, and stud, being played by the individual, encourages that freedom of expression so desirable if all participants are to enjoy an evening's entertainment. Of course, your thoughts on the subject are your own!

Often it is much better strategy to play the caller than to play the original bettor. As long as your cards are "tops," or so long as an opponent must have more than he has showing to beat you, naturally you are justified in staying, unless the betting becomes burdensome due to increased bets and raises.

Do not encourage others to stay in a pot with you just to try to beat some player who has displayed strength. Every contestant should play his own hand, and two persons should never have identical interests in the same pot. Do not indulge in post-mortems; they do no good and quite often encourage you to try experiments on subsequent hands that are unsound.

Some poker philosophies and principles are based on a "lying and lying in wait" policy. The author has always believed that "a quick quarter is better than a slow dollar," so is inclined to take the viewpoint that aggressive playing is the sounder of the two ideas.

Build up your own pots. If the boys show an inclination to try to outdraw you when you have a good pair, backed, charge them for the privilege. Do not get the idea that in the writer's opinion competition is not desirable. It most certainly is and is very necessary; but make competition pay its way.

To play a "waiting game" when you have a large pair "back to back," hoping that your opponents will raise and re-raise the pot just so you can win big stakes, is a negative line of thought. It certainly is presumption of the cards' mercy, as it were. You have to treat the cards properly, play them correctly if you want them to win for you, and "sitting on them," inviting disaster, is the eighth "deadly sin." Laws of compensation hold good in stud poker just as in daily life, and if your opponents want to play against your aces, kings or queens, make them pay for their education. You probably paid for yours.

If players with aces, kings or queens in the hole insist on trying to outdraw your jacks, backed, discourage the pernicious practice by making the vice expensive. If you do not charge them for the privilege they will probably take it for nothing. Of course, if you are sitting in a spot where you are advantageously located, with a powerful hand and other players show a desire to increase the pot's value, you should give them plenty of encouragement by merely "chipping along," or calling until the time comes for you to display your power.

Even though you bet aggressively, this does not mean that all your opponents will lay down, but you will at least cause some of them to withdraw, and it certainly is better in more ways than one to win a pot with four or five stayers than to lose one with seven or eight opponents in it.

A singular feature about games of skill and chance, particularly when played among friends, is that toward the end of the game the losers very often desire to raise the limit. In most cases these losers are actuated by a "double or nothing" complex, but merely a little thought on the subject will enable these players to understand the futility of the idea, insofar as its relation to winning or losing is concerned.

In most cases a player is losing because of two main factors—he is either playing the game poorly or is receiving poor cards. And sometimes, a combination of both circumstances.

How can a change in the game's limit remedy this situation?

The only reasonable solution to the problem is this: resolve to lose only so much at any one time, then stop playing. This procedure will solve the main difficulty of probably 75% of poker players.

Another feature about stud poker that no previous plan of attack or defense will be able to overcome is the fact that oftentimes a player, although starting with the best hand, will be outdrawn by some opponent. The question is, just what can be done about it? Obviously, the answer is: nothing.

Any player who objects to some opponent's trying to win any particular pot by legitimate methods has no business playing stud. He should be playing some game that does not require the mental alertness that this game demands. Also, do not cultivate the idea that all the other players are "ganging up" on you. Every player is for himself, alone, and it certainly is no particularly pleasant satisfaction to Bill Smith to know that Izzy Cohen outdrew Mike McCarthy one time in a stud game. "It buttered no parsnips" of Bill's, especially when Mr. Smith was in the game at the same time, and leveling, too!

Play your hands in such manner that when you are outdrawn your losses will not be great enough to overcome your winnings in the normal course of play.

It would be almost impossible to codify the rules in poker to the extent that has been done in bridge, as in bridge good cards can hardly ever be made to yield to bad ones, except in cases most extreme. In poker there is "a battle of wits," with the ultimate winners usually being those who have studied the game from psychological as well as from mathematical angles.

In bridge, a player cannot control card distribution; the art in the game is in skillfully bidding and playing those cards that have been dealt you. In poker, a different procedure is maintained, as to a great extent card distribution can be controlled. The art in stud poker consists in playing or "betting up" those cards that you have received or in dropping out of the betting, thus virtually controlling distribution, when the cards that have been dealt you are, in your opinion, worthless. This idea of participating or not, born of one's own volition, is a singular feature about poker that certainly enhances its merit as a mental exercise.

Poker also differs from bridge as equity differs from law, and surely the Chancellor, the "Keeper of the King's Conscience," that "Avatar of Wisdom" is every whit as respectable as the most eminent of the advocates before his bar of justice. Poker also differs from bridge in the idea of being one against all and all against one; but notwithstanding, a camaraderie is engendered, an amity is bred, that more than compensates for the possible "sense of loss" suffered by those who like games of a partnership nature. Being "on your own" has a tendency to prevent congelation of thought and lethargy, both incompatible with success in any venture.

Stud poker is a game that is fast in execution and requires fast thinking if it is to be played successfully.

One reason why, in the great majority of friendly games (and all games should be friendly), no one wins or loses much oftener than another is because the great mass of stud players play the same kind of game. The vast majority of poker players care little about the laws governing the immutable design of the warp and woof of any martingale. They seem to get more of a thrill in outdrawing an opponent than in making an adversary pay in an unsuccessful attempt to outdraw them.

Probably the most successful stud players are those who never show their hole cards unless they are called, nor make any unnecessary showing of power. Merely display enough power to win; do not show your hole card unless necessary; let your opponents guess the hidden secret of your ability, if they can.

No writer on the subject of cards can tell you, personally or individually, just "how to win at stud poker" every time you play, so in order to qualify this book's title at least one comment is necessary, and it is this: not everyone who plays this system will invariably win, as sometimes you will pair your king in the hole just when your opponent pairs his ace— and your opponent may also be playing "according to Wickstead."

I firmly believe, however, that the great majority of consistent winners will be found playing the game as described herein; and as poker players are a hardy lot, you will not find around the stud table any ano- dynes to assuage the wounded feelings of a loser. This may not be the most "sociable" way of playing stud poker, but it certainly is productive of results. The theories and principles in this book, constituting the Theory of Probability in its application to stud poker, to a great extent, bear the same relation to the game that actuarial tables bear to life insurance, with the exception that actuarial tables must be revised from time to time to keep pace with improving living conditions which influence life expectancy. The ideas set forth in these pages are everlasting in their accuracy and will be correct so long as two and two make four. Their application to stud will be admitted as long as there is an enlightened man in the world.

In the chapter "A Short History of Cards in General and Stud Poker in Particular" I mentioned a certain peculiarity about the court cards in the pack, which, in my opinion, deserves thought to a far greater extent than it has received in the past. I refer to the fact that some of the court cards are shown in profile.

A discussion of this oddity belongs more properly in a chapter devoted to the philosophy of cards rather than in one dedicated to their history, as it emphasizes the truth of the idea, namely, that the original concept of cards was that they should be used to convey certain ideas and messages allegorically, instead of being used merely as counters in a game of chance and skill.

In her book "The Devil's Picture-Books," published in 1890, Mrs. John King Van Rensselaer says, "Why it is that the Knaves of Hearts and Spades should be in profile, while the others show their full face, will probably always remain a mystery; but it may be observed that the Knave of Hearts is in the same position in some very old packs now preserved in the British Museum, to which has been attributed the date of 1440."

This premise brings up interesting speculation, and the facts contained might be due to the theory that playing cards are both enigmatic and esoteric, and herein probably lies the reason for the jacks of hearts and spades, and the king of diamonds also, being shown in profile only. A deeper reason exists for these truths than to attribute them merely to the whim of some long-forgotten artist.

In the gradual evolution of our modern card, it is generally agreed that the heart suit represents love; clubs, power; spades, death; diamonds, wealth. Kings represent manhood; queens, womanhood, and jacks, youth. Of the four kings, the king of diamonds alone is shown in profile.

Incidentally, in some old packs the king of diamonds wears no crown. But he is Caesar, isn't he? And if you remember your ancient history, Caesar was no king and therefore had no crown. The battle axe carried by the king of diamonds represents the fasces, emblem of authority of imperial Rome. The king of diamonds also faces the emblem.

I wonder if the artist who drew the originals intended to temper mysticism with cynicism by illustrating the fact that the one insatiable desire that man has is his search for wealth, his greed for gold? Man turns from death, as witness the king of spades, and he is only lukewarm toward power, as evidenced by the king of clubs.

Man is not insensible toward love, however, as shown by the doughty king of hearts, facing the emblem with sword raised, ready to strike for his queen; but wealth alone seems to be the only loadstone with power sufficient to merit all of man's attention.

Womanhood, represented by the queens, seems to be only mildly interested in those things for which the suits stand, even though the queen of spades does turn from the death sign.

For those "in the springtime of life" the jacks of hearts and spades exemplify the two features most consonant with youth, namely, its desire for love and its horror or fear of death. Youth seeks no power, as the jack of clubs tells us, and it does not seek wealth to any great extent, as proven by the jack of diamonds. The action of the jack of hearts in raising to his lips a symbol before bestowing it upon his inamorata proves that youth is always eager to prove its affection for its "light o' love." The jack of spades turns his head from the death sign to a far greater extent than do the king and queen, proving that youth clings to life far more tenaciously than does age.

Craving for love, or the creative instinct; fear of death, or self-preservation; greed for gold, or the profit motive! Is this the equilateral triangle containing within its perimeter the summa that epitomizes the story of the ages? Is this the secret that some schoolman desired to lock up in what he thought would be an impregnable "donjon keep," there to be kept "forever and a day"? I leave the answers to you.

In a chapter devoted to the philosophy and ethics of stud poker, it is no more than proper that a reference to the morality of card playing should also be made. When man first discovered that he could distinguish between "a short straw and a shorter one" the desire to gamble or bet was born, and there is no evidence extant to prove that this craving is possessed by any other creature.

Everyone, irrespective of station in life, environment or heredity, has his or her idea regarding the morality of actions indulged in or contemplated, so let's look at gambling in its generic sense, and particularly in its relation to those things in everyday life as well as in its relation to cards.

One of the instincts or inclinations with which man has been endowed, in contrast with the lower animals, is the propensity for gambling. It is one of the by-products of creation and is peculiar to man alone, as it represents a function of that power of the soul which we call the will. Memory and understanding in practically all their plenitude are shared by animals as well as by man, but the attribute of will power is man's alone to have and to hold.

When Du Chaillu, the first white man to see a gorilla, came upon the great anthropoid, the big ape might have been soliloquizing on any number of things. For instance, the susceptibility of the children to colds, or possibly his love life was not up to par, or maybe he was having a hard time making a living; things held in common by man. But you can "make book" that he was not reproaching himself for having tried to fill an inside straight the night before, nor was he chattering about having played a deuce in the hole at a stud session. Nor was he offering "two to one, no four."

We might define gambling as the staking of money or other thing of value on the issue of a transaction or game of chance, in which the loss or gain depends on an uncertain event over which the participant has no control. But gambling is an inclusive term and, although often used in an exclusive sense, can readily be applied to almost everything that occurs which has any element of uncertainty regarding its final end.

Moralists commonly require four conditions so that gambling may not be illicit. "1st. The amount staked must belong to the gambler and must be at his disposal. 2nd. The gambler must act of his own free will. 3rd. The game or transaction must not be fraudulent. 4th. There should be some sort of equality among those participating in the scheme to make the contract equitable." You can easily see from the foregoing conditions that a rich man wagering, say, $100.00 on a horse race or investing $1,000.00 in cotton futures may be breaking no moral code, while at the same time similar investments by a man of lesser wealth might constitute the gravest of crimes.

Among some people the term "gambling" has a most sinister connotation. Oftentimes these same people will rail at some game of chance or mingled chance and skill even though the four conditions mentioned before are present in their entirety, and at the same time freely invest, possibly beyond their means, in some so-called business speculation so tainted with fraud that it ceases to possess the right to be considered at all by honest men.

Why should there be more moral obliquity attached,

say, to a game of cards, per se, than to investing in the grain or produce markets? Especially when the grain and produce are bought solely as a speculation. The individual in the stock market does not have nearly as much control over his investment as that possessed by the participant in a game of chance and skill. And again, the investment of the individual in a game of chance and skill represents a larger percentage of the total amount involved than is represented by the investment of the individual in the stock market. Therefore, it would be more in conformity with the natural law to presume that he could protect his stake to a greater extent.

Furthermore, the case in behalf of the morality of stud poker, in contrast with stock market investing, can be made much stronger when you consider the fact that there are no fictitious values created in a stud game. In a poker game, when a total of $10.00 is lost, the same total is won by the winners in the game, but this is not true in stock market speculation.

An investor worth $50,000 on Monday may see this value shrink to $10,000 in several days, but this loss does not necessarily result in corresponding gain for other speculators.

I realize that the game of poker is not hallowed or sanctified by making the point, namely, that plunging in the stock market is just as bad from a moral viewpoint. My contention is that there is no moral turpitude involved in either case when indulged in merely to the extent of one's means.

For one to say that he cannot play the game as set forth in this book is not a true statement, because only the will is involved; and the will knows no "can" or "cannot." Of stud poker it may be said that it belongs to that phase of human activity which can truthfully be called contemplative, and therein lies its spirituality.

Heretofore, all the argument, both pro and con, on the game has been done around the table, "in chambers," as it were; let's bring it out before "the bar of public opinion" for a final decision, and with this thought in mind I rest my case.

To us, the true lovers of stud, the dulcet, rhythmical cadence of the falling of the cards creates a diapason to which but few things can be compared. Orphean-like in its efficacy to charm the attentive ear and capture the receptive mind, this "music of the spheres," as it were, sounds like the dreamy tinkle of a cowbell wafted o'er a field of blue-bonnets at the close of a halcyon summer day.

Nor does it require much expansion of the imagination to hear, in this unique symphony, the honeyed euphony not unlike the voice of a loved one, the cooing of a babe, or the harmony begotten by the falling of a feather "dropped from an angel's wing."

Technical Terms Used in Poker

Adversary—opponent, competitor.

Ante—the original stake for which you play.

Bobtail—a four-card straight or flush.

Case Card—the last card of a denomination.

Duffer—one ignorant of the game's principles.

Inside Straight—one broken in the middle, such as 3-4-6-7.

Kitty—the percentage taken out for expenses.
Limit—the maximum bet that can be made at any one time.

Mis-deal—failure to distribute the cards properly.

Pot—the stake for which you play.

Punter—one who plays against the banker.

Round—when all players in the game have had their chance of betting.

Shuffling—mixing the cards so that all traces of previous arrangement are lost.

Stock—cards left in the pack after completing deal, for use in following play.

INDEX